THE INCREDIBLE LOU FERRIGNO

HIS STORY

With His Step-by-Step Training
Program and Special Techniques
for Building a Superb Body

LOU FERRIGNO

and

DOUGLAS KENT HALL

Simon and Schuster

NEW YORK

ALSO BY DOUGLAS KENT HALL:
On the Way to the Sky
The Superstars
Let 'Er Buck!
Rock & Roll Retreat Blues
Rodeo
Van People: The Great American Rainbow Boogie
The Master of Oakwindsor
Body Magic

WITH ARNOLD SCHWARZENEGGER:
Arnold: The Education of a Body Builder
Arnold's Bodyshaping for Women

EXERCISE PHOTOGRAPHS BY DOUGLAS KENT HALL

Copyright © 1982 by Lou Ferrigno and Douglas Kent Hall

All rights reserved
including the right of reproduction
in whole or in part in any form
Published by Simon and Schuster
A Division of Gulf & Western Corporation
Simon & Schuster Building
Rockefeller Center
1230 Avenue of the Americas
New York, New York 10020

SIMON AND SCHUSTER and colophon are trademarks of Simon & Schuster

Designed by Stanley S. Drate

Manufactured in the United States of America

10 9 8 7 6 5 4 3 2 1

Library of Congress Cataloging in Publication Data

Ferrigno, Lou.
    The incredible Lou Ferrigno
        1. Ferrigno, Lou.   2. Weight lifters—United
States—Biography.   3. Deaf—United States—
Biography.   4. Bodybuilding.   I. Hall, Douglas
Kent.   II. Title.
GV545.52.F47A34   646.7'5   81-23226

ISBN 0-671-42863-2   AACR2

To my wife, Carla,
and our beautiful daughter, Shanna Victoria,
and to my mom, dad, and family

TITLES WON

1971   Teenage Mr. America
1973   Mr. America IFBB
1973   Mr. Universe IFBB
1974   Mr. International IFBB
1974   Mr. Universe IFBB

I am grateful to all the people who have played a part in my career as a bodybuilder and an actor. I am indebted to Gold's Gym, World Gym, and the Sports Connection for allowing me to use their facilities for photography. And for their generosity and support during both my career and the making of this book I want to thank Joe Weider, Tim Kimber, Art Zeller, John Balik, Craig Dietz, Ken Sprague, Joe Gold, and Universal Studios.

We would like to thank the following for permission to use photographs:
Joe Weider, *Muscle & Fitness Magazine,* and Artie Zeller, pp. 2, 3, 6, 63, 69, 75, 90, 91, 97, 105, 112 top, 114, 207, 208
Jimmy Caruso, pp. 81, 82, 83, 84, 85, 86, 87, 88, 117
Craig Dietz, pp. 60, 61, 89 bottom, 94, 95, 96, 103 top, 144
John Balik, pp. 89 top, 98, 101, 106 bottom, 107, 112 bottom, 133, 134, 135, 136, 137, 138, 139, 140, 141, 142, 143, 146, 147, 153, 154, 155, 156, 157, 158, 159, 160, 161, 162, 163, 165, 166, 167, 168, 169, 170, 171, 172, 173, 174, 175, 176, 177, 178, 179, 180, 181, 203
Bob Gardner, pp. 104, 151
Marvel Comics and Universal Pictures, pp. 92, 93, 115
CBS Television and Tony Espanza, pp. 77, 78
Mike Sullivan, pp. 9, 10, 51
Ed Jubenville, pp. 68
Color photographs courtesy of Joe Weider, *Muscle & Fitness Magazine,* and Jimmy Caruso, Bob Gardner, and Richard Roecca

Jacket photographs courtesy of Joe Weider, *Muscle & Fitness Magazine,* and Jimmy Caruso, John Balik, and Doug Hall. And with kind permission of Marvel Comics and Universal Pictures.

PART
ONE

1

It was almost midnight when I pulled out of the lot at Universal Studios. We were a full day behind the shooting schedule on an episode of *The Incredible Hulk* and nothing seemed to have gone right since early morning. All I could remember was being in makeup before eight o'clock that morning, unable to touch myself or lie down in my motor home between scenes for the next fifteen hours. Everything had been crazy—a wall had collapsed on the set; one of the stunts had not worked. We had another early call for the next day and I wanted to get home and catch some sleep.

On the freeway, I moved into the fast lane and pressed down on the accelerator. I had driven less than half a mile when I heard a siren and saw red lights flashing in the rearview mirror.

"Dammit!" I pulled over and got out of my car fast. Two cops leaped from the patrol car, taking cover behind the open doors, their pistols drawn. I couldn't believe it was happening—it had to be a joke.

"Don't move," one cop shouted, crouched, both hands on his pistol. "Turn around, put your hands against the car, and spread your legs."

"What's this all about?" I started to turn toward them.

"Spread 'em!" the cop shouted, poking his gun at me.

"Okay, okay. Take it easy." I was shaking.

One kept his pistol on me while the other frisked me for weapons. "He's clean."

"Let's see your driver's license."

"It's in my wallet."

"Where's your wallet?"

"In the glove compartment."

"Get it—but try anything funny and we'll shoot."

They kept me covered while I got my license out of the car. One cop examined it in the headlights and handed it to the second. "It's Lou Ferrigno!" The second cop started jumping up and down, beating on the hood of the patrol car. "It's the Hulk! I don't believe it." Suddenly they wanted to be friendly, to shake hands.

I asked them why they had pulled their guns.

"The way you came out of that car we didn't know what we had. We were afraid we'd need to protect ourselves."

They wanted my autograph. I made a deal with them. I would give them each a signed photograph if they let me go.

"You've got it!"

After I had signed the photographs, the first cop said, "I'd be careful if I were you. The way you jumped out of your car I wasn't sure what we were going to have to do to stop you. I was hoping you weren't drunk and crazy, because the thought that kept running through my mind was that even this gun wouldn't have done any good."

I could attribute this recognition to my role as the Incredible Hulk, but this wouldn't be quite right. Everything I have achieved, including my success in television, came through my efforts as a bodybuilder. I am never sure what people think when they see me. Do they realize the hours I put into training, the countless tons of iron I moved to make this body? Do they know that bodybuilding was instrumental in helping me overcome disadvantages that other people accept and allow to circumscribe their lives? Seeing me as a child, nobody would have guessed that one day I would become one of the biggest men in the history of professional bodybuilding.

Training was like the start of a new life for me. I no longer felt the urge to shut myself away in my room the way I had as a kid. I had found a sport I could do and not worry about what anyone else said or thought. It came complete with a new and almost private language. A rep was a repetition; a set was an uninterrupted series of reps of a single exercise. There were plates and collars and bars and special machines for every exercise. Lats were short for lattisimus dorsi and made up part of your back, pecs were your chest muscles, and abs were the quilt of muscles that ran the length of your stomach. No one could keep me from exercising or force me to play the worst position on the team—because there was no team. Now I never needed to worry about being rejected or left out.

Bodybuilding became my escape and my key to survival. I went home at night and worked out all the frustrations that had accumulated during the day. I spent hours in the basement, training, expressing my feelings. I watched myself in the mirror and fantasized about someday bulging with muscles, becoming a great bodybuilder, a movie star. At that time being really big was merely fantasy. I was only average height and I was skinny as a pole. I had no trace of fat or obvious muscle on me anywhere. It was a hard time for me. I was starting into my teens. I wanted girls to look at me, to notice me and be attracted to me, but with my awkward body and the hearing aid I needed to wear, I felt like the Elephant Man. I wanted attention so badly I was motivated to train harder than ever. It was during this period that I developed the discipline and the burning desire to succeed that were eventually to carry me to the top of the bodybuilding world and into the entertainment business.

Me with some of my first trophies

But those accomplishments were a long way off. I worked and worked, putting in rep after rep of my exercise program to try to achieve some change. I was obsessed; I wanted my biceps to burst out and be as peaked and hard as baseballs. But I had to learn to wait; I had to learn patience.

After about four months of grueling work I suddenly had arms. It happened just like that. I got pumped up one day and hit a pose before the mirror and there they were. I did a few more quick reps with the barbell and raced up to the living room. "Ma, Dad, look at this!" I struck a double-arm pose for them, checking myself in a mirror we had on one wall.

"That's terrific, Louie," my father said.

"Why do you want to do this to yourself?" my mother asked. "You spend too much time down with those weights."

"It's good to be in shape, Louie," my father said. "But if you put the same amount of effort into your studies that you do into lifting weights you could be a doctor."

"I don't want to be a doctor, Dad," I said. "I want to be a famous bodybuilder."

When I was a kid my friends called me names. Tin Ear, Deaf Louie, anything that made fun of my problem. "It's the Deaf Mute," they'd shout. "Hey, Mute!" That word used to make me burn, but I would never fight. I wasn't big as a child, and most of the time I hung out with older guys I didn't have the courage to challenge. I had never been a fighter. I felt weak inside; I was afraid of being hurt. The few times I did lose my temper and take a poke at a guy I ended up with a bloody nose. Once I even had the ear mold yanked from my ear—leaving me awash in silence. Fighting had never done any good. The other guys just used that against me too. "Hey, Tin Ear . . . Deaf Louie! Come on, let's bust the Mute's hearing aid!"

They would all dance around, hitting at the bulge under my shirt where the hearing-aid box was strapped to my chest.

"Stop it!" I tried to keep their blows from landing on the hearing aid and sending an explosion of sound to my head. "If you break it, you'll have to pay. It cost more than a hundred dollars!"

As a child with my hearing aid

As a baby I had had a series of severe ear infections. The doctors tried everything, but the infections didn't clear up and the nerves in my ears were permanently damaged. Still nobody figured out that anything was wrong until I was four years old. I didn't talk—except to say "Momma" and "Daddy" and a few other words that weren't very clear. People used to tell my mother not to worry, that Albert Einstein didn't speak until he was five, that boys in general were slow in learning to talk. The pediatrician said the same thing: "Don't worry, Mrs. Ferrigno. Look at him—he's a healthy child." Nobody thought about a hearing problem. There had never been anyone in our family who had had one.

Then one day my mother read a newspaper story about a little boy people called the Wild Child. He was bright and mischievous, and he appeared to understand a great deal, but he would not speak. He was slow at learning sounds. He seemed to have slipped into his own private world. Somebody told his parents it could be his hearing.

My mother came back to my room, where I was busy playing with my toys. She stood behind me and clapped her hands—just as the woman telling the story had. I didn't jump or turn around. She tried again—two, three times—until she was convinced I did not hear her. An ear specialist confirmed her suspicion: I had suffered a severe hearing loss. Irreparable damage had been done to both my ears.

The doctor fitted me with my first hearing aid, a box I had to wear on my chest with a wire going up out of the collar of my shirt to a buttonlike mold that twisted into my ear. I hated it. It was ugly and strange and made me self-conscious, and it seemed to embarrass the kids around me. I found every way possible to avoid being with people. I spent a lot of time in my room alone, looking at my books and playing with toys. I could not listen to the radio, but I did watch TV—often with the volume all the way down, watching only the picture.

In spite of the fact that I hated being seen wearing the hearing aid, certain sounds I had never heard before getting it fascinated me. I developed what my mother called a humming habit. I would cup my hand over one ear and make one of the sounds I liked. I would hold it for a long time. It was a way of entertaining myself as well as a method of learning sounds and forming new words.

The worst thing about the hearing aid was what it did to me psychologically. I hated to have people know I wore it. It frustrated me and caused me to do odd things. I wanted to wear clothes which would cover the wire. I would try to keep my head turned so people could not see the button. A number of times I actually pulled the mold out of my ear and stuffed it down into the neck of my shirt to hide it.

My refusal to deal with the hearing aid realistically was not a problem confined to childhood. It was only three years ago that I was finally able to talk about it publicly, that I was willing to let people know I wore a hearing aid. For more than twenty years I attempted to hide both the hearing aid and the fact that I needed it. And this worked a serious hardship on my image. People either concluded that I had a severe speech impediment or—more often, and more to my disadvantage—that I was just a big, slow bodybuilder.

I'm certain that the hearing aid and the difficulty I had communicating with people ultimately had a great deal to do with my becoming a bodybuilder. In those first years of school I shut myself in my room, away from the kids who teased me or refused to include me in their play, and I spent hours daydreaming. I admired men of incredible physical strength and development, men who could under extraordinary circumstances accomplish superhuman tasks.

My father took me to a big bookstore in Brooklyn and bought me stacks of comic books. I always chose characters like Superman, Spider-Man, and the Incredible Hulk. The Hulk was different in the comics from what he became in the series, but I was impressed by his being a loner and a doer of great deeds.

I would lie under the window in my room and read comics until I had memorized the stories. I loved the idea of being huge and using all that power for good. I saw myself being chosen to play these roles in movies and becoming famous. In fact, that was probably the beginning of my interest in acting. It was a desire that would always be with me, even though shyness and extreme self-consciousness would prevent me from attempting to pursue it in school. Still, in a strange way bodybuilding would make up for that by giving me a real taste of the professional stage as well as creating the body and the power of concentration necessary to make the transition into the part of the Incredible Hulk.

My parents hated to see me isolate myself in my room. They tried everything to motivate me, to interest me in things that would draw me out of my shell. Fortunately, they did not pity me, and they would not allow me to feel sorry for myself. I think part of the reason for this is that my father refused to believe I was in any way handicapped. He came from an old-fashioned Italian family, and we lived according to the same strict Italian family code he'd grown up under. He always considered things better if they were done the hard way. If he acknowledged I had a problem—and I suppose he did—he just figured it was something I had to work hard to overcome. He expected me to act normal—in spite of the circumstances. He never showed any sympathy toward me or gave me any special privileges. If I misbehaved he got out the belt. To this day, I respect him for that. If it had not been for his pushing me, urging me to be with new people and do new things, I know I would not be what I am now.

I think the most frightening and frustrating experience for me was starting school. My father would not consider sending me to a special school for handicapped children. I don't believe my parents even discussed it. We were Catholics. He enrolled me in St. Athanasius, a parochial school at 51st Street and Bay Parkway in Brooklyn.

The first-grade teacher seated us in rows according to the alphabet. As luck would have it, I ended up at the back of the classroom, where it was almost impossible for me to figure out what was going on. My hearing aid was effective only as long as I could also read the lips of the person speaking to me. With this combination of sight and sound I could just barely get along. But I was too shy to tell the teacher I needed to be close. In fact, I tried hard to pretend there was nothing wrong with me, to hide my hearing aid. The teacher was a nun and a stern disciplinarian. I think she thought I was stupid, or from another country and just starting to learn English, like many other children in that section of Brooklyn. She would ask me a question, and either I wouldn't know she was talking to me or I couldn't hear what the question was.

Finally, my parents realized what was happening. They went in and talked to the mother superior as well as to the nun who taught my class. They moved me to the front row, and I was able to begin to participate. But I would always have this problem. I had to watch the teacher constantly to *see* what she was saying, and in later grades when tests were based on class notes I didn't do as well as I could have because I could not watch the teacher and take notes at the same time.

It was at about this time I began attending classes conducted by the New York League for the Hard of Hearing. There I was taught the techniques of lip reading and how to form different sounds. At the end of each class the instructor would read a story, making certain we could study the lip movements that went with the sounds of each word. It was slow and tedious, but it helped. I felt more comfortable in my classes there than any place else and found myself reaching out and making an effort to communicate.

I went twice a week to night classes and attended a session each Saturday. My father was a policeman in a Brooklyn precinct. It was hard work and he put in a lot of hours, but he always tried

My father in his policeman's uniform in Brooklyn

to arrange his schedule so he could take the train with me when I went into Manhattan to the New York League. He would wait outside the classroom, and when class was over I would usually find him asleep in the chair. Part of our routine on class nights was to go downstairs to Woolworth's, where he would buy me a Brick, my favorite kind of ice-cream sandwich. Then, on the train home, he used to laugh at the way I ate it. I savored every bite. I bit off the corners and then continued nibbling around it in a circle until I had eaten it down to a chunk no bigger than a half-dollar. It was almost painful to swallow that last bite.

Even in those days my father had an interest in bodybuilding. He would often buy a muscle magazine to read on the train in to the city or back to Brooklyn. Together we would look at the photographs of these men with their incredible builds. I would tell him that his muscles were almost as big. Bodybuilding became something we both liked, something we shared. My father did not joke around very much, but sometimes when I stopped at the open bathroom door to watch him shave he would spin toward me and hit a pose. "Hey, Louie, how do you like that chest?" I thought he looked terrific.

My parents worked tirelessly at helping me with my speech when I was home. My father was a very hard man. He was constantly after me about my enunciation of different words, and he would persist until I showed some progress. He never allowed me to get sloppy, no matter how tired he was or how exasperated it made me.

"Louie, you've got to learn to speak right," he'd insist.

"I'm trying, Dad."

"Well, try harder."

When he finally reached his limit and became so upset he started to shout at me, my mother would come in from the kitchen and stop us. She was the peacemaker in our family, a role she would be forced to play more and more frequently until I moved out of the house when I was in my mid-twenties.

Thinking back, I realize that my mother has been a saint, a rare and generous soul. I have never seen her lose her temper or be unkind. She is, I believe, the kind of woman who would have made a great nun.

Many times I quarreled with my mother. I was tired, I didn't want to study, I wanted to watch TV instead of going in to the New York League for my lesson. "Louie," she would encourage me, "you've got to do it. You can't let down." She stuck with me right to the end of everything, always ready with help and encouragement. That's what I love most about her.

I remember once bringing home a report card with a couple of low grades. I was disgusted with myself and said I didn't want to learn anymore. "You just have to try that much harder, Louie. Later, you'll need your education. You'll see. You can do better."

It was an entirely different story when my father, who had a quick Italian temper, saw the report card. He exploded. "Oh my

God," he cried. "What's wrong with you? Look at these grades! You can't get anywhere in life with grades like these. You'll be left out. Think about it. Who will ever hire you? It's going to be tough enough being hard of hearing."

My father was a big man and looked even bigger in his blue police uniform. I liked looking at his muscles when we joked around. But when he was angry he frightened me. My mother knew this, and when things cooled down she would come to my room and tell me that was just the way my father was; it was something I had to learn to accept and live with. "Go talk to your father," she would say after he and I had had one of our differences. "He feels bad when you fight."

I had to be the one to make up, because my father didn't seem to know how to say he was sorry. I never heard him apologize—to me or to anybody else. He has always been a hard and stubborn man, as bullheaded as they come. Which did not keep me from admiring him. I realized these were the principles by which he lived and that he did not waver from them. And my mother always told me that no matter what happened, what he did or said, I was to respect him. It was from her I learned the gift of giving in.

My father's anger wasn't limited to report cards. Like most kids in our area of Brooklyn, I used to love to play stickball. My friends and I would gather in the street after school and play until dinnertime. Once when I was at bat and a low pitch came across the plate I swung at it as hard as I could and lost my grip on the bat. It went flying up in the air and crashed through a third-story window. A woman started screaming. I thought I had killed her. I took off running down the street and hid in the laundry room in our basement. A few minutes later I sneaked up the stairs to a window. A woman in a bathrobe and a scarf was coming toward my house surrounded by all the other kids. The stick I'd thrown had broken her bathroom window and flown right into her bath. The kids stopped and pointed at my house. I felt the sting of betrayal and slipped back down into the laundry room and turned off my hearing aid.

My mother listened to the woman's story and then came to find me. She woke up my father, who was working nights at the time. He pulled the black belt from his pants. Standing there, he looked bigger than when he stopped shaving to pose for me or when he was in the basement working out with his weights. I was spanked, sent to my room, and forbidden to play in the street for two weeks.

The day I was allowed to go back into the street to play was another disaster. I stood down on the corner, bouncing my ball against a building and waiting for the other kids to come out of their houses. I was challenging myself by trying to hit a three- or four-foot area of bricks between the first- and second-story windows. One throw fell short and the ball shattered another window.

"Louie, Louie," my mother cried, wringing her hands, "I'm going to have to wake up your father." She hated it as much as I did.

It was during these first years of school that the term "the outside world" became fixed in my mind. My life was divided into two areas: There were the safe zones, which were inside my house with my family or at the New York League for the Hard of Hearing, and there was the outside world, which was the world I encountered when I went out on my own, when I went to school, when I went into the street. The outside world was fascinating and frightening. I wanted to be a part of it, but I wanted to be someone else when I was out there. Those were the times when I hid my hearing aid and did everything else possible to prevent people from finding out I was handicapped or from treating me in a special way. I tried to pretend I was like them, another person on the street, ordinary, normal.

There was one two-week period when the horror of the outside world became very clear to me. It was the first time I had ever gone away from home alone. I took a bus with a group of other kids to spend two weeks at Camp Grant in the Catskill Mountains. The camp had been designed to give kids from the city a firsthand taste of being away from their families and living in the outdoors. The major activities were hiking and boating and almost every kind of outdoor sport.

Life at camp was not easy for me. In some ways not being able to hear and speak normally had left me years behind. I was insecure about striking out on my own. I had become a follower, because it was easier. I put too much trust in people. I modeled my life on what I saw in my parents and friends and failed to develop the independence that matched the kind of person I really was.

This became obvious at camp, and it frustrated me. I felt lost. I went in whatever direction the other kids went, making every possible attempt to be part of the crowd. This annoyed the other guys, and they bullied me and tried to cut me out. I tagged along anyway. I was afraid to do anything else.

The only time I slipped off on my own was to go to the shed where the sports equipment was kept. There was an athletic instructor at the camp who worked out with weights at a certain time every day. I discovered this during the first week and started showing up at the shed to watch him. I asked him why he lifted weights. While he went through his routine, he explained each movement and how it affected particular muscles. He said that it was his favorite sport, that he was training for competition. This came as a surprise to me. My father had a set of weights in the basement, but I had never connected the kind of training he did with sports; I thought it was something he was required to do because of his police work, as essential as his stick and gun.

The camp instructor explained that weight training was a serious sport, much older than games like football and baseball, and that a person could do it and become huge and muscular and gain international recognition. Most of the words he used, such as "vascularity" and "definition," were over my head. But I was impressed by his stories about various Mr. America and Mr. Universe contestants and his talk about Steve Reeves and other body-builders who had become movie stars. It fit the pattern I had envisioned for myself.

I had begun to feel a desire to be noticed, to gain recognition for something I had done, some feat of strength, some unusual accomplishment. I immediately identified with bodybuilding. Not the least appealing aspect of it was that I could train alone. Never again would I be sent to right field or told to wait on the sidelines until someone else was unable to play. And although it would be at least a couple of years before I began to train with seriousness and dedication, the hours I spent talking with that instructor at summer camp and watching him work out helped awaken me to body-building as a way of life.

It was harder for me to understand what was going on at camp than it was at school, because a great deal of the instruction and most of the announcements were given over loudspeakers. There were no lips to read, and the kind of harsh garbled sound that came from the speakers was reduced to a meaningless roar in my head. To be on the safe side, I attached myself to a group of boys and followed them through the parts of each day when I did not know what we were supposed to do. Certain activities were just impossible. For instance, when we gathered around the campfire to sing, I could never figure out what the words were. I would sit and move my lips a little, trying to mimic the others and hoping no one would notice I didn't know the songs.

During the hour when my group went down to the lake for swimming instruction I would wade out only so far and then return to the shore. I could not swim. I had never learned, using my hearing aid as an excuse. I had a fear of water, compounded by the fact that my hearing aid would be damaged or ruined if it got wet. I didn't dare take it off. First, there was the embarrassment of having the other guys see it, and second, I was afraid I would miss more than I was already missing.

Today, the hearing aid is no longer a problem. I go to the gym and take it out before I begin to train. I don't care who sees me. I am not afraid to tell people to speak up, that I don't hear well. That may sound strange, but all my life I felt that the box on my chest or the small receiver hidden behind my ear was hideous. Even at home I took off my hearing aid in the bathroom where no one could see it. Finally, I realized that I should not care, that I was allowing it to cripple me, that I should let other people know I wore a hearing aid and read lips. I felt as if I had been let out of a cell. At the same time I decided to wear two hearing aids. What an incredible difference! I could finally hear whole sounds, complete words. I realized that I was speaking in the same muffled voice I had always heard, and I began to reeducate my palate muscles so I could duplicate the new sounds I was hearing. However, that was a long time after the two weeks I spent at summer camp. For fifteen more years I would live under the shadow of fear and shame.

One day there was a big hike planned for the entire camp. I

kept my hearing aid on all during the night before the hike, because we were getting up early and I did not want to miss the wake-up call. Sometime during the night my batteries went dead and I failed to hear the loudspeaker. Later, I jumped out of bed and saw that everyone had gone. I was so upset at having been left that I dressed quickly and raced off in the direction I thought the others had taken, forgetting to put new batteries in my hearing aid. I walked and walked along the trail, choosing new trails when I encountered a fork or a crosstrail. After a couple of hours I had to admit to myself that I was lost. Nothing looked right to me. I didn't know what to do. I turned and tried to find my way back, wandering from trail to trail, unable to remember which ones I had taken.

At some point during the morning the camp instructors figured out that I had been left behind. When they couldn't find me in camp, they started a search, and by late afternoon they had called in the police. Search parties kept combing the forest, calling for me, vehicles circled the forest roads, honking, but I couldn't hear any of it. My hearing aid was useless.

It began to get dark. I had not eaten all day, and the forest started taking on frightening shapes I did not want to see but could not help looking at. I huddled under some trees until finally I fell asleep.

The next morning the police found me wandering through the forest. They had a hard time understanding what I kept trying to say to them. I was frightened and cold and hungry, and they thought I was in shock.

That fall when I went back to school my fifth-grade teacher put me in the back of the classroom. No one had explained to her about my problem, and I still did not have it in me to tell her I needed to be close. It was not long before my grades began to plunge. They dropped to where I was barely passing. Then I failed an important geography test.

The teacher spoke with my father on the phone. She told him I seemed unable to keep up with the other students and suggested I should be sent to a public school where the work would be easier. He was disappointed, but he thought maybe she was right and public school might be better for me. He got in touch with the principal of the school and arranged for me to be admitted.

My teacher at public school was a man with a reputation as a strict disciplinarian. He had little patience and showed no one any favors. Everything was new, and again I was too shy to tell him to put me in the front row, close enough to read his lips. The second day he asked me a question, and I didn't respond. He repeated the question. Everyone in the class looked around. I thought he was talking to someone behind me, so I looked around too. "Ferrigno!" he shouted. "I'm looking right at you!" The kids started laughing, and I ducked my head.

A few days later my teacher called my father and told him he was having trouble with me and asked him to come in for a conference. When my father explained to him that I needed special attention, the teacher said point-blank that I should be sent to a school for the deaf. They were equipped to deal with those problems. My father got furious, but I could see from the look on his face that under his outburst he was genuinely hurt. He went to the mother superior at St. Athanasius and asked if I could have another chance. The mother superior spoke to my former teacher there, and it was arranged, once more, for me to sit in the front of the class. "Louie," the mother superior said to me before I left her office, "you must learn to speak up. You must tell people you need help."

"I will, Mother," I said. I wanted to, but inside I wasn't sure I could.

What happened afterward made that one of the greatest days of my life. When I walked back into the classroom the other kids stood up and cheered. They had actually missed me, and realizing that did more for my self-confidence than anything I could have experienced. I sat in the front row, my grades improved, and from that moment on I began learning how to be strong within myself.

2

We had weights in our house on 5th Street before I was ever born. My father bought a basic bodybuilding set—barbell, a few plates, and a pair of dumbbells—in order to get in shape for the agility test rookie candidates had to take before they were allowed on the New York Police Force. He trained hard every day for six months, and when he took the test he made a perfect score, something he spoke of with pride. He continued to work out all the time I was growing up. He had never been educated in bodybuilding, but he knew a few basic exercises and they helped him keep fit.

After the summer-camp athletic instructor talked with me about weight training I began paying more attention to my father's workouts. When he was in the basement, I would go down and question him about each of the exercises. Although his knowledge was limited, he took the time to tell me all he could. It was generally true of my father that he would do anything to encourage my interests, anything to keep me out of the isolation of my room. Once when he saw how much I liked to watch him work around the house he went to the hardware store and bought me a bag of assorted plumbing fixtures—short pipes, elbows, tees, and straight couplings. Like most boys, I was interested in how things were made. I had stripped down my toys and taken apart two kitchen chairs. The plumbing fixtures were new and I think intended to save the furniture from destruction. Using my father's wrenches, I played with them for hours and hours, building toys, creating structures that looked like buildings or vehicles. Then one day I noticed that the radiator had the same kind of pipes and couplings going into it as my father had bought for me. I stared at it for a long time, wondering how it made heat. I pushed aside the pipes I'd been given to play with and carried my father's tools to the radiator. It took all my strength to break loose the first joint. I worked and worked, watching the teeth of the wrench bite into the pipe and the threads slowly worm out of the coupling. Suddenly, the radiator seemed to explode in my face. Hot water shot out all over the place. My mother ran into the room, screaming. Luckily, my father, who was working nights then, was back in the bedroom. He was able to race down to the basement, turn off the water, and fit the pipes back together. But not before a great deal of damage had been done—there is still a mark on the ceiling of the dining room from where the water first spurted up and left a faint rusty stain.

As I grew older, power, strength, and a whole range of super-human deeds occupied my mind more and more. I had been through all the comic-book heroes. I knew their stories by heart. In fact, every comic I had ever gotten from my father was in my room, stacked in my shelves, in perfect condition. Superman and the others were no longer enough for me. I wanted to know more about real men of strength. I wanted models. Because of this I was able to remain close to my father. No matter how tough on me he was or how much I would sometimes curse him under my breath after he lost his temper and punished me, I admired him. He was strong, and being a policeman gave him a certain power, a certain stature. I knew the people in our neighborhood respected him, and I was proud of that.

When I told my father I wanted muscle magazines instead of comics he worked out a trade with our newsstand owner. I carried in a stack of comics in mint condition and brought home a stack of muscle magazines. Each time my father thinks about that exchange today he reminds me that it lost us a small fortune. But I didn't lose a thing. For weeks afterward, I spent all my spare time in my room, reading and digesting every bit of information between the covers of those magazines. I knew exactly where to find every article on any particular body part or the latest workout routines and secrets of all of the great California muscle stars. I read every word, all the ads for training equipment, the announcements of the big championship contests. I was as meticulous about the new muscle magazines as I had always been about my comics. I kept them in perfect condition. And it exasperated me when my father would come in to see something I'd asked him to look at and he was rough with the magazines, bending them back double in order to read the page.

After a few weeks, I started explaining to my father exactly what happened when he did a certain exercise—how the Bench Press built up the pectorals, how Curls peaked the biceps, how Chin-ups developed the back. His attitude about training changed. He added a couple of new exercises to balance his workouts. But there was still a humorous tone in his voice when he would say: "Hey, Louie, look at this one." He would turn and show me a standing lat spread, flexing until the V came out right down his back.

The simple set of weights my father had bought had been adequate for his purposes as a policeman, but my dream was to set up the basement like the gyms I saw featured in the magazines. I did errands to earn extra money for the new equipment we needed. My Uncle Joe, who was in the oil-burner business, had a client who sold sporting goods; Joe made a deal for some weights at a big savings. I was in heaven the day he drove over with the stuff in his trunk.

24

I went immediately to work on the room in the basement. I found an old mirror back in a closet: It had a crack running right down the middle, but I drove in a nail and hung it on the wall anyway. I knew from everything I had read that all the professional gyms had mirrors so you could watch yourself work out, practice posing, and spot-check your progress. I think this was the aspect of training that frightened my mother the most. She came downstairs to see the new weights Uncle Joe had brought over and saw me working out in front of the mirror. "Louie, what are you doing?"

The look on her face was enough to tell me I should ignore her question. "Someday, Ma, I'm going to be so big, so strong, you won't believe it."

"I just hope you know what you're doing."

I kept on exercising, using the new weights, trying all the techniques I'd worked out from the magazines. The next morning my muscles would be so stiff I could barely move, and they stayed sore for days. But I didn't care. I couldn't wait for school to let out in the afternoons so I could hurry home and start working out.

At first my training was limited almost entirely to the arms and shoulders, the showy muscles that would give a skinny guy some size. I knew people were starting to notice me, and I began wearing T-shirts everyplace. One night when my three cousins, three girls, were at my house, they started to tease me. "Come on, Louie," they coaxed, "take off your shirt." Finally they talked me into it. I sucked in my stomach until it was hollow and flexed so my biceps and deltoids popped up. The girls became absolutely silent. I could see they were impressed.

The winter I was sixteen and attending Brooklyn Technical High School, which is a special high school for boys who want to pursue careers in some aspect of engineering, my workout sessions did become a problem. I had really slacked off in my studies, and although I knew what the result would be I couldn't help it. I was interested in only one thing—bodybuilding. As usual, the crisis came when my mother insisted that I had to let my father look at my report card. When he saw my grades, he hit the ceiling. He drove off to the hardware store and returned in less than half an hour with a heavy steel chain and a padlock. He chained all my weights together and fastened them with the lock.

"All right, young man, when I see some improvement in your schoolwork I'll unlock those weights—but not before."

I had never been so depressed. My mother came to my room. "He means it, Louie," she said. "You won't get pity from your dad. You know that. Once a cop, always a cop. But that doesn't mean he doesn't love you."

The next afternoon, I sneaked into the basement, took a hacksaw to the chain, and cut through a link that would free my weights. I worked out for a couple of hours and then put the chain together so no one could see it had been cut. At the end of the week my father discovered what I had been doing. All hell broke

At first I worked mostly on my arms and shoulders

loose. He came out of the basement screaming my name at the top of his voice: "Louie!" He wanted to kill me.

My mother stood between us and talked him into calming down. Finally we made a deal. I would be allowed so much time each day in the basement with the weights and then I had to go to my room and do homework. My father promised that if my grades improved I could spend more time working out. On the next report card my grades were back up to passing.

I don't think anyone realized how serious I was. Bodybuilding became my religion, muscle magazines my Bible. Each day on my way home from school I stopped at the newsstand hoping to see a new copy of *Muscle Builder Magazine.* When I finally did see it on the rack that meant a wonderful evening for me.

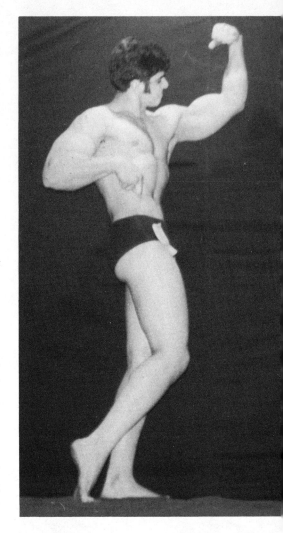

I was careful never to tell my folks when I got a new magazine. I would slip it between the history and English books in my briefcase. Then after dinner I would say, "Okay, Dad, I'll be in my room doing my homework." About an hour later my mother would make her routine check on me. I would hide the magazine under my looseleaf. "How's it going, Louie?" "Fine, Ma." I tried to look as if I was struggling through an assignment until she left. I perused the muscle magazine thoroughly, the way I never did my legitimate studies, turning the pages slowly, devouring every word. I would end up having to hurry through my lessons at ten o'clock that night. But I always did them well enough to pass, to keep my workout privileges. After the incident with the lock and chain I knew my father meant what he said.

Guys at school still made fun of the way I talked, and now they added to that the fact that I was always lifting weights. But it didn't matter what they said. Inside me had sprung up a desire they could not discourage nor kill. Sometimes I would get fed up and argue with them, but I was never good at arguments and in the end I would get discouraged by it all and just walk away, thinking: Someday they'll be sorry, someday they'll want to be my friend.

If I took one of my magazines to school, which I often did if I hadn't finished a particular article the night before, the guys really razzed me about that. "Hey, Louie," someone would say, "how come you're always reading those faggot magazines? Why do you want to look at men's bodies all the time? You got a problem?"

"We hear you got no girlfriends, Louie," another guy would say.

I attempted to laugh and act as if I didn't care what they said, but I was not yet strong enough to keep from being hurt by this criticism. The one thing it did was to make me train harder, and that put me closer to my goal.

It wasn't true that I didn't like girls. I was simply too shy and socially backward to do anything about it. There was a girl I had a crush on who was also hard of hearing. I had met her in the night session I had attended at the New York League. I got up the courage one night at dinner to mention that I might take her out. "But Louie," my father said, "she's hard of hearing." I don't know if he ever realized how that statement struck me.

Later, my cousin Barbara, who was my age and came to the house regularly to help me with my lessons, did fix me up with her girlfriend Chris. I kept saying I wanted a date with Chris but I couldn't get up the courage to ask her. Finally, Barbara got us together and said, "Louie wants to ask you out." There was no backing down then. I asked if she wanted to go bowling the next Saturday. I still remember the way she replied: "I'd love to," she said.

For a couple of days I was too excited to tell anyone. Finally, trying to be casual, I mentioned it to my folks.

"Hey, Louie's got a date," my father teased.

Then I was sorry I'd said anything. "Come on, Dad, lay off. It's only to go bowling."

"Look at him blush."

"Come on, Dad."

"Matty," my mother cautioned, "don't."

My mother pressed my slacks and shirt. "Do they look all right, Louie?"

"Yeah, yeah, Mom. Great. They look great."

The closer the time came the edgier I grew. What would I say to her? Sometimes when I talked to people it made them uneasy because I had to watch their lips all the time they talked. How would she be affected? I tried to put it out of my mind. I must have combed my hair a dozen times before it got slicked back into the Elvis Presley style I liked. My little brother Andrew was no help; he kept peeking in the bathroom or in the bedroom and I would drive him out, trying to hit him. Then my mother started asking about the girl: Who was she, what was her family like? "Look," I cried, "it's only my first date. You make it sound as if I've been going out with her for a couple of years."

"Take it easy, Louie," my father said. He winked at my mother. "Here, here's five bucks extra—in case you need it."

When I reached the girl's house it took a minute to get up the courage to knock on the door. Her mother answered it. "Hi," I said, "is Chris in?"

"No," her mother said.

No? I couldn't believe it. Her mother said she had gone out with some friends to see a movie.

That sent me into an incredible tailspin. I just stood on the doorstep while Chris's mother shut the door. I couldn't bring myself to go back home. I didn't want to find any of my friends. I walked around the streets aimlessly. I stopped in a store and flipped through magazines. I tried to drink a Coke. Then—there was nothing more to do. The minute I stepped into the house my father looked at his watch. I sat down. They seemed to know what had happened, but neither of them said anything. When I was able to get it out, my mother was sympathetic. "Don't worry about it, Louie," she told me. "Don't worry about it." My father said it was only the girl; she didn't have any class. I knew it was more, but I didn't know what to do about it. I changed clothes and went to the weight room in the basement, hating even the sound of my feet on the steps.

After that, I really narrowed my focus in on weight training. I had already made significant gains. My shirts were starting to fit tight across the shoulders and chest. My mother mentioned that maybe they could be let out; I said no, I liked them that way. "Louie," she cried, "what's come over you? This muscle business has gone to your head."

She was right. I thought about nothing else. My heroes were all bodybuilders—Larry Scott, Dave Draper, and Arnold Schwarzenegger. My idol was Larry Scott. I kept a scrapbook of my favorite guys in their best poses, and there were more photographs of Larry Scott than all the others put together. He had incredible charisma and finish. He was perfectly proportioned, and his posing style was elegant. In all of the photographs his body had the perfection of polished stone.

I remember the first time I saw Larry Scott. It was 1965. He had already won Mr. Olympia. He was to defend his title at the Brooklyn Academy of Music. The day before the contest a bunch of guys from my neighborhood were standing around rapping about Scott and how great it was going to be to see him in person. I flexed my bicep and said, "See this arm? It's shaped just like Larry Scott's. One day it's going to be larger than his. It's going to be the biggest arm in the business."

One of the guys said, "One, two, three—" And all of them joined in with a "Ha, ha, ha." The first guy shook his head. "What a fool you are, Louie." Was I?

That night, upset with my friends, I went to the contest alone. I showed up early and stood beside the stage entrance where I could watch all the bodybuilders arrive. They looked like giants. They were huge and incredibly cut. At first I'd taken off my jacket and was standing around in a T-shirt. But pretty soon I felt so intimidated I put my jacket back on and tried to be inconspicuous. Seeing photographs of the bodybuilders in magazines was one thing, but it had not prepared me for the real bodies. And they hadn't even gotten pumped or anything yet.

I slipped inside. It was fantastic to see all these famous bodybuilders. I stared at them, studying them from every angle; I checked arms, chests, backs, legs. I had never seen legs like these pros had. It was something young guys—including myself—totally neglected. And later when Larry Scott came onstage, forget it. Seeing him was like seeing a god. I sat transfixed all through his routine. He was powerful, cut, defined, and he moved with all the grace of a dancer. The applause was thunderous; people stood and cheered until he came back. He got the best ovation I ever heard.

28

Me at seventeen

After the contest I made my way through the crowd and hurried back around to the stage door. I wanted one more glimpse of Larry Scott. When he did walk out a few minutes later he seemed to glow. He was shaking hands with people and signing autographs, but I was too shy to step up and offer either my hand or a scrap of paper. For days, I couldn't get his image out of my mind. I kept seeing his blond hair and golden tan. I had been inspired in a way that was difficult to explain. I was convinced more than ever that that was the life I wanted.

Scott's example encouraged me to begin training more than just the upper body, more than the arms and shoulders and chest. I started doing Squats and Chins for my back. With my father's help I expanded the basement gym, moving from the laundry room, where it had begun, until it occupied the entire basement.

About the age of seventeen, when most people had reached their full stature, I began to really grow. Scientists might argue with me, but I like to think this came as the direct result of my incredible desire to become the biggest, most famous bodybuilder of all time. Suddenly, I grew inches taller, put on size, and began to add layers of muscle. As exciting as my new burst of growth was, it came not totally without problems. The basement had been adequate for workouts when I was ordinary size. Now, as I shot well over six feet tall, each time I did a standing French Press or Dumbbell Triceps Extension, the weight would crash into the ceiling. I remember my father running downstairs, swearing. "Look at what you're doing! Look at that ceiling! Jesus, Louie!"

"Dad, I can't help it if I'm tall."

"You're going to knock down the house."

There was nothing else he could do, so he started lowering the floor of the basement. We broke out all the concrete and dug down another foot, carrying the dirt out in buckets and hauling it to a vacant lot bit by bit in the trunk of our car. We cemented pipes in the floor for machines and benches and installed wood paneling around the walls. We replaced the old cracked mirror with a better one. My father had a leg-press machine built for me, and I made a couple of exercise benches. We cut corners whenever we could, because my father's salary from the police department wasn't that great. Still, in the end, I had the best home gym I've ever seen.

It was during this period that I saw Arnold Schwarzenegger in person. There were two international contests being held that same day at the Brooklyn Academy of Music—Mr. Universe and Mr. Olympia. And Arnold was competing in both of them.

Because I had grown so much and would eventually have to compete in a different class, I had gradually shifted my preference from guys like Larry Scott and Dave Draper to Arnold. Arnold had made the way for the tall man in the sport. He proved that a good tall man could beat a good short man. He broke down the prejudice against the tall man and opened the door for people like me. In fact, Arnold was in the process of taking bodybuilding into areas where it had never been accepted, and that made seeing him even more important to me.

I went with my father to the Brooklyn Academy of Music. He was a sergeant in the same precinct where the Academy of Music was located. He asked to see the manager, showed him his badge, and talked to him for a minute, and we were allowed passes to go backstage.

"Louie," he said, stunned, "they're like gladiators."

I stepped into the room where Arnold and a number of other bodybuilders were pumping up. I stood in a corner and watched Arnold, taking in each move he made. This guy from Austria's big, I thought to myself, but I'm taller and someday I can be even bigger than he is. I fixed those ideas in my head and let my mind go to work on them. I noticed that as Arnold was pumping up he glanced at me out of the corner of his eye. I wondered if he had any idea what I was thinking. There were a lot of questions I wanted to ask him—but I could not get up the courage.

"Louie," my father said, "I'm going to get Arnold to pose with you for a picture."

"Don't bother him, Dad." I could see that he was involved with the contest and very nervous.

"I mean it, Louie. I want you to have your picture with him."

"No, Dad—"

Arnold got up from the exercise bench and started for the door.

"Arnold," my father said, "could you just hold it for a minute and pose for a picture with my son?"

"Later," Arnold said. "Not now, later on."

My face burned. "You shouldn't have done it, Dad."

"Louie," my father said, "someday I hope you're on the same stage with him."

I hoped that too, but not for the same reason.

That night, Arnold won the Mr. Universe but he lost the Mr. Olympia title to Sergio Oliva. That didn't matter to me. Arnold was the first superstar I had ever seen in person. His appearance on stage under the lights was much more impressive than backstage. He seemed bigger. He radiated confidence. You felt it in every move he made. Each pose was more spectacular than the one before.

In Arnold's example I saw what my potential as a huge bodybuilder could bring me. A big bodybuilder could be graceful and elegant. In the basement gym, during lunch hour at school, any time I had a spare minute, I would find myself staring off into space, caught up in a daydream. I thought how great Arnold must feel stepping out onstage, seeing all those flashbulbs go off, people freaking out, holding on to the curtains and crowding the police to try to get onstage. It had only been like that until he hit his right-arm shot; then nobody in the audience could move. Over and over again, I said to myself: I want that feeling. I thought about it so much that from that day on I never slacked off my training.

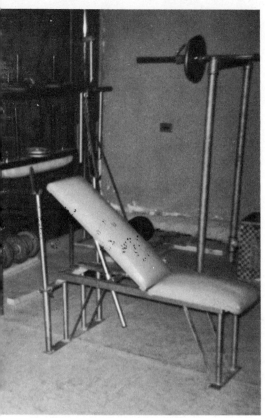

The gym in my basement
where I first worked out

A few months later my father promised he would take me to the Weider factory to get me a new bench and some Olympic plates which I needed for my increasingly heavier workouts with the bar. The night before we were to go to the factory I was too excited to sleep. Ever since I had started reading *Muscle Builder Magazine* I had been studying Joe Weider's full-page ads for equipment and dreaming of owning a complete barbell set. That night, each time I closed my eyes, I pictured the factory, a place full of machines and weights.

We left Brooklyn just after noon. Out of New York we got on the New Jersey Turnpike and my father said to watch for the Desoto Avenue exit. As we were driving my father said, "Louie, I'm starting to worry about you. All this weight training, weight training. Your mind's on nothing else. When you're older, it's going to give you some problems."

"I'll be all right, Dad." I kept counting the exits, determined we wouldn't miss Desoto Avenue.

"But Louie, you can't support yourself with bodybuilding."

"Don't worry, Dad." But I could see he would.

"Dad, this is the exit."

When we pulled up to the warehouse I saw a black guy with huge arms walking around the yard. He turned around and I realized it was Bill Grant. I'd seen him in Weider's magazine. I walked up to him and said, "Wow, what a pair of arms you've got." I asked if he'd come out to see the equipment. He said he was working for Joe Weider. It seemed like the best job in the world, being around all those weights and machines.

Harold Poole—another star from the magazine—was working inside. He took us through the warehouse. I kept thinking that someday I wanted to buy everything possible for bodybuilding— every kind of weight, every kind of machine. That was my idea of heaven. Guys I knew talked about owning a Stingray or a Trans Am but there was nothing I loved more than the look of all that iron or the feel of the gnarled handhold on a seven-foot Olympic bar. It meant more to me than a car or anything else.

Besides the bench my father had promised he would buy two 50-pound plates and two 35-pound plates. I said I would load them in the car. I slid the bench in the back seat. I put the four plates in the trunk, and I could see my father still in the office taking care of the transaction. So I just kept on loading. I made another six or seven trips to the iron piles. When I saw my father and the guy from the office coming out I slammed the trunk lid. The guy looked at how low the car was sitting. "Springs don't look too good," he said. "You'd better take it easy." That was an understatement—the gas tank was touching the springs.

My father gave me a funny look. But he got in and we drove away. I didn't say much during the trip home. We pulled into the garage. When I opened the trunk and my father saw what I had done, he blew up. Weights were coming out all over the place. "Louie, I'm a cop, for chrissake. I arrest people for doing this!"

Then he broke down and we started laughing about it, though later the weights got returned.

My father had been right to worry about my future. From his point of view it didn't look all that great. I was plodding along in school, just making average grades, and I had no outside interests except bodybuilding. My own view of school was to get it over so my life could begin, but I didn't know exactly what I meant by that. My attitude toward the guys who still teased me and tried to bully me had changed. I was a lot stronger now, and I got into a few fistfights. I had never enjoyed fighting, but now I could win, and that stopped a lot of their teasing and snide remarks. They may have continued to call me Deaf Louie and the Mute, but they didn't dare do it to my face.

In the lunchroom one day someone talked me into an arm-wrestling competition. Nobody could beat me. It was, in a strange way, my first taste of notoriety, and I loved the feeling it gave me. I already had 17½-inch arms, and I liked the way people looked at them.

In my senior year I met another bodybuilder from Brooklyn. He was a year older than I and was really huge and muscular. He had a construction job, lifting heavy beams and doing rough work. He inspired me to start building up, putting on more weight, increasing my muscularity.

He took me to R&J Health Club for the first time. I had thought I was getting big, but by comparison, the guys I saw in R&J were animals. I was not intimidated by them, just as I had not been intimidated by Arnold. However, I felt a competitive urge I had never experienced at home in my basement gym, where I worked hard but always within the limits of comfort. I realized that training alone was not going to be enough. I needed more. When I met Julie Levine, the owner, and told him I wanted to be a professional bodybuilder, he recognized some potential in me and offered to let me train at the gym free. Julie gave me some valuable advice. He pushed me and encouraged me. That was a real boost to my ego, but I took with me to the gym the same old problems I'd had all along. I didn't want anyone to know about my hearing aid. I took it off in the locker room and then worked alone—because I couldn't hear anything anyone said to me.

Most of what I learned came from just watching other bodybuilders, from trial and error. Often, in fact, when I saw someone performing a new exercise I would wait until I completed my workout and then I would go home and try the new exercise in my basement gym—before I attempted to do it at R&J.

It was an entirely new experience to train around other people, professionals who spoke the language I was struggling to learn. I liked it and I didn't like it. They tried to include me, but I felt inadequate and shied away, keeping to myself. I realized that if I was to succeed I had to learn to be around other bodybuilders, to learn from them and be inspired by them. Most of all, I knew I had a long way to go.

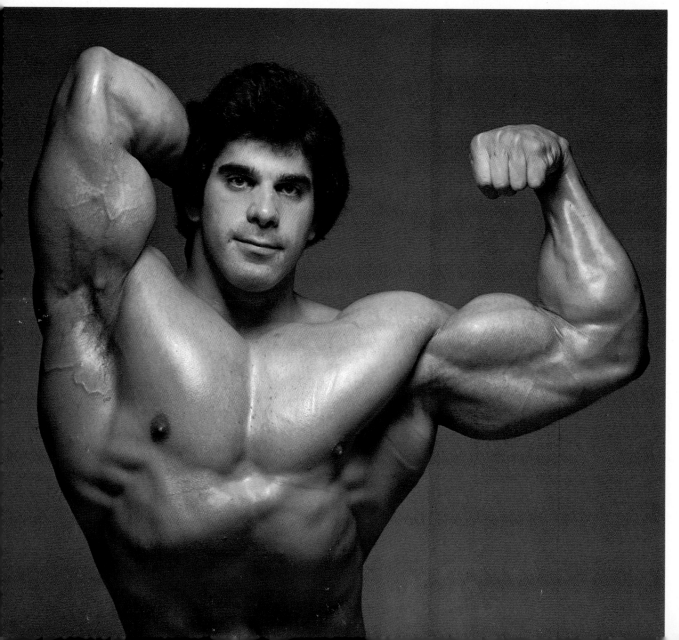

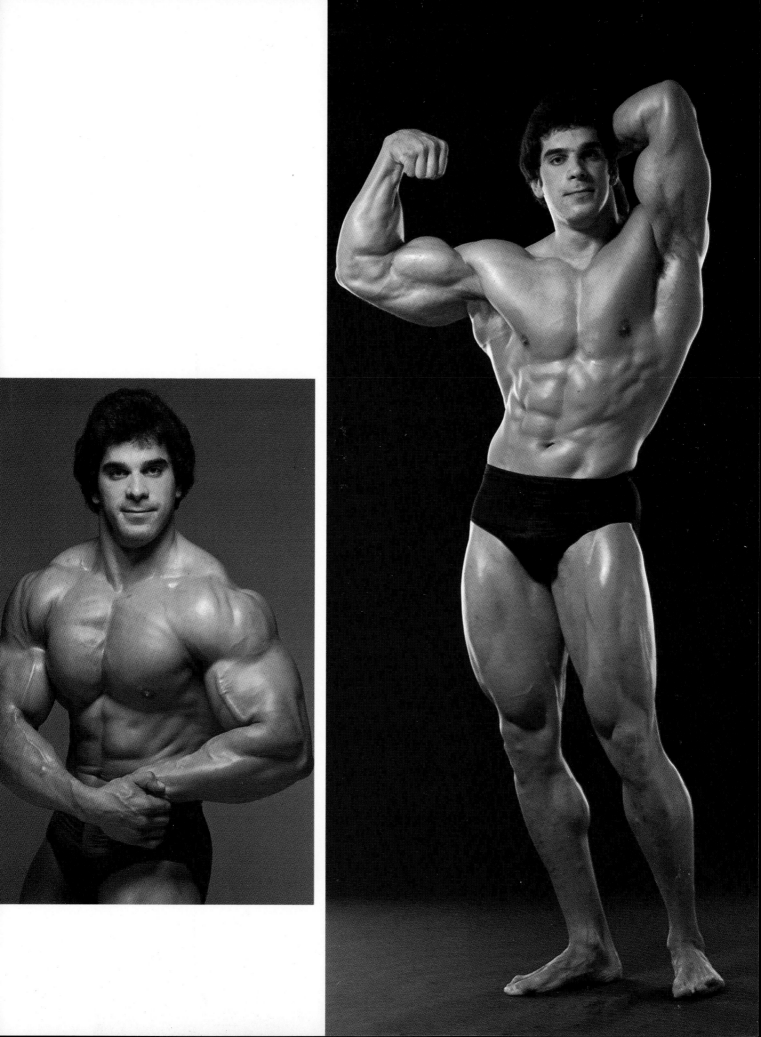

3

Two significant things happened about the time I graduated from Brooklyn Technical High School. I decided I was good enough to begin competing in bodybuilding contests, and my father decided it was time I got serious about a career. I had been brought up to respect my father's wishes, and I accepted his advice and help in looking for a job. Fortunately, the Sheet Metal Workers Union, which up until then had been virtually closed to outsiders, had just been forced by a court action to accept minority applicants. I took the test and, thanks to my training at Brooklyn Tech, scored in the top hundred out of three thousand applicants. I got an apprentice card and went to work at New York Sheet Metal in Brooklyn. I wasn't convinced this was the career I wanted, but I had always been gifted with my hands and I liked working with tools and building things. In fact, in less than six months I was operating machinery on my own, which for an apprentice was almost unheard-of in the trade.

My father kept saying what a terrific career sheet metal was. It is true, I was earning good money, but I refused to look at it as a career. To me, it was merely a way to get through a couple of years until I could exist on my earnings from bodybuilding.

As soon as quitting time came at New York Sheet Metal, I stopped at the gym, where I put in a good workout before driving home to eat dinner. After that I went to the basement and trained some more. Now that I was working, my father's enthusiasm for my bodybuilding returned. He seemed to think of it as a hobby. He kept helping me install the new equipment I bought for the basement. We found a guy who had a small equipment factory not far from where I worked. We hired him to make a leg machine tailored especially for me. I had the day off and spent it at the factory watching them cut and weld the machine together. After we set it up in the basement, there was only one problem: It sat right under my grandmother's bedroom. I wanted to try it out, but it was after eleven o'clock and she had gone to bed. I couldn't force myself to wait until the next day, so I sneaked down, loaded it lightly, and started doing some slow reps. The machine felt great; it had a terrific smooth action, with the work going directly to the muscle. That excited me. I piled on more weight, and did a second set.

Then I really loaded it up. I was just starting to get a pump when the door opened and my grandmother, who was a pretty feisty old woman, shouted down the stairs: "Will you stop it with those goddam machines! For chrissakes, it's midnight. What's the matter with you!"

I acted as if I didn't hear. She muttered something else in Italian and closed the door.

I added another 50 pounds. Then I added another 50, bringing it up to 400 pounds. I'm not sure what happened, but when my legs were all the way extended one foot slipped. The whole 400 pounds came crashing down. It cracked like thunder, knocked my grandmother out of bed, and woke up the whole house. The jar had cracked the plaster in the ceiling and blown the overhead light. I was lying there in darkness, listening to the sound of everybody running downstairs.

Finally my father got a light turned on. He saw me lying there, not injured, and he really started to scream. He was a policeman, he cried, he worked hard all day; was it too much to ask to be allowed a decent night's sleep once in a while?

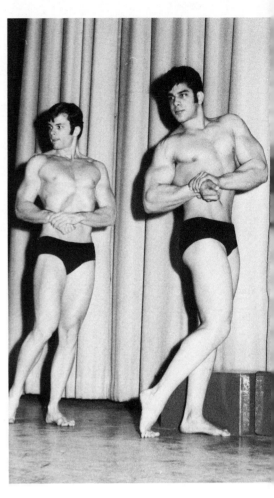

Having a great house was one of my father's passions. He was always working on something, adding a new improvement. He fixed up the walls of the basement with new, expensive paneling. When he finished he begged me not to go near the paneling with any of my weights. He didn't want it marred or scratched. "Okay, Dad, I promise I won't touch it."

One evening I had gone downstairs to do some work on my chest and shoulders. By then my grandmother had stopped yelling at me. I had brought her into the basement a few times to show her what I was doing. She had admitted she could see progress in my body, and I think she respected my dedication, though the whole phenomenon of bodybuilding and why I was doing it puzzled her. Later, when she began to see me on TV, she would become a fan, but at that time she only tolerated it. That particular evening I did something no bodybuilder should ever attempt. I put all the weight I could possibly handle on the bar and began doing Bench Presses without a partner. I completed 10 reps, decided to go for 12, lowered the bar, then couldn't get it up. The bar pressed against my neck, making it difficult for me to breathe. I was in a spot where I couldn't throw the bar sideways. I thought: I've got one choice, over my head. I struggled to get the bar high enough and threw it back over my head. Before it hit, I knew what I'd done. I heard the crash and turned in time to see the plates break right through the paneling.

My father wasn't home, but my mother came running down to see what had happened. She nearly fainted. "What do I tell your father, Louie?" In the end, she lied to him, telling him the electricians who had come in to work on the lights had had an accident and had given her a few bucks to repair the wall. That saved my neck.

I think I was nineteen the year Sergio Oliva won the Mr. Universe. For months I had been reading about Sergio's training, the advances he had been making. Dave and a couple of other friends were going to take the train in to the prejudging. I had bought my ticket the first day they had gone on sale, and I wasn't going to miss the event for anything. Subway trains ran from our station every hour. At ten minutes to eleven we ran down the stairs to buy our tokens. The man was not in his booth. This was not one of the bar-type turnstiles. It went floor to ceiling and you had to have a token to get through. We could already hear the train coming. I was getting frantic. Someone said the train was stopping at the next station. I ran over to the fence, grabbed two of the steel bars, and tried to pull them apart. At first nothing happened.

"It's coming!" yelled one friend. "The train's coming!"

I strained. The bars moved.

"He's doing it!"

"Come on, Louie," Dave said. "Think of who's going to win the contest. Think of Sergio."

I strained.

"You're getting it, Louie. Just a little more."

I could see the headlight on the train now. It was slowing into the station. No way was I going to miss seeing Sergio. I shut my eyes and called up every ounce of strength I had. Sergio, I whispered to myself, Sergio. The bars moved a few final inches. We barely squeezed through the opening in time to run to the train.

Later I felt a little uneasy about what I had done, but I was determined to get to that show!

Naturally, I admired all the big bodybuilding stars. I had a desire to be like them, to be famous, to be featured in the magazines; but the person directly responsible for getting me into competition was Dave Strasser, who had taken me to R&J. I had met Dave my last year in high school. Walking home one afternoon we began talking about weight training. He stopped and showed me his arms, how he'd peaked his biceps and brought out all three heads of his triceps. I was impressed. My arms were bigger, but his had a finish I was a long way from achieving. At the time Dave was training for the Teenage Mr. America contest, and the way he talked about it, his attitude and his desire to win, awakened the competitive spirit in me. If he can do it, I thought, I can too.

At the gym I started talking about competing—about entering contests and winning. "Sure, Louie," the guys all said, "you'll knock 'em dead." That negative tone made me train harder; I added weight, did more reps. They could not discourage me. I kept trying, and I kept believing I would be great. That kind of believing and acting upon my belief became a ruling principle in my life. Even today, when I really want something and I believe I will get it, it happens. It's almost an automatic thing. I used to daydream constantly about being the kind of person I am today. In my mind I saw myself living the kind of life I do. My belief was so strong that it came true.

The first bodybuilding contest I entered was the Mr. New Jersey Open Hercules Competition in Trenton, N.J. A few weeks before the show I started putting together a posing routine. I remembered a series of images from the big contests I had witnessed—the Universe and the Olympia. I drew poses from them, from photographs in magazines. I got criticism from my father, from my friends, and from Julie Levine at the gym.

Three friends and I drove to Jersey in my VW. As a start, I got lost in Trenton and couldn't find the hall where the contest was being held. We drove around for almost an hour before we finally found it.

I had been pumping up my ego for days. At nineteen, I was six feet five and weighed 215. I couldn't imagine anyone in an amateur show beating me, which revealed the depth of my ignorance about the sport in those days. But when I walked into the building, my confidence took a dive. I saw all these bodybuilders already beginning to warm up for the competition, doing towel pulls, Push-ups, working with barbells and dumbbells. They looked fantastic. I remember being overcome by a sinking feeling and saying to myself: "Oh, man, Louie, you've got so much work to do." I was big, bigger than anyone; but I was raw and uneven. I had almost no development in some areas, not to mention any real finish or definition.

From what I know about competition now, I realize that my attitude at that moment—the acceptance of failure—cost me at least fifteen places. I was not prepared in many ways—I had a pair of old trunks and a shabby bathrobe—but I was least prepared in my mind. These other guys seemed so confident—they had that even when they didn't have the body to go with it. They oiled themselves up and strutted around like real pros, flexing, stopping to check a pose in the mirror. I was a nervous wreck. The reaction of the other competitors to my body helped bring me back around. I was big and had a few impressive points, such as my arms. I could see them checking me out.

My hopes took another boost from the audience. When I hit my double-biceps pose, which was to become my most famous pose, they whistled and screamed. It was the first time I had been onstage, the first time my physique had been applauded. I began calculating how I would do with the judges. Maybe fifth or sixth, I thought, seventh at the worst.

It was staggering when I heard the results. I had placed twenty-second. It struck me so hard I did something crazy and totally impulsive, something that up to that time I would never have dreamed of doing. I walked up to the winner, shook his hand, and said: "One or two years from now you'll be second place to me."

My doubts returned when I was back in the car. I laughed and joked with my friends, but under all the humor I was seriously going over the contest in my mind. I thought about all the training I had done, the points I had neglected strictly out of vanity. I concluded that now it was all or nothing. Either I was going to give up or I was going to give it all I had.

My father had waited up for me. They were sitting at the table, just the way they had been the night I came home from being stood up on my one and only date. I sat for a long time without saying anything. I hated to tell my father I had come in in twenty-second place. He said, "Don't worry, Louie, it takes time. You're young. You can do anything you want."

I was in no condition to go up to bed. I went down to the basement and sat on a bench, looking at all the equipment we had put together. And it was not a question of what my decision would be: I knew I would give bodybuilding everything I had. I went back upstairs, where my folks were still talking. I could tell they were concerned. "Dad," I said, "I'll never come in less than third place again."

From that day on I trained like an animal. I doubled my time in the gym. I decided to get bigger than ever and started really bulking up, eating nine meals a day, packing on pounds. The guys at work who had once joked with me about my muscles and all the talking I did concerning contests I wanted to win stopped joking. They acted frightened of me and I'm sure they thought I'd gone out of my head.

I admit it was a weird time, and the things I did were pretty funny. I brought my lunches in a shopping bag—there was that much. I hung a whole bunch of bananas in my locker so I could peel off one whenever I wanted. On coffee breaks I ate a couple of sandwiches, and I stuffed in more at lunch. If I got hungry in between I said I was going to the toilet and I sneaked a sandwich in the stall and ate it there where the foreman wouldn't see me.

Packing on that much mass and muscle was not without its problems. My food bill skyrocketed. I estimated that just what I ate was costing over $170 a week (this was ten years ago!). I was forced to buy custom-made clothing. My mother helped me here. Since my senior year in high school she had been making special shirts for me. It was typical of our relationship that she would choose some patterns and fabric samples and we would discuss them. She had become an expert at taking the biggest available patterns, expanding the arms and shoulders, and then tailoring the waist so it had a great fit, even on a body as exaggerated as mine.

My second competition was the Mr. Wagner Contest. My preparation and approach were totally different now. I had restructured my training program. I had more sophisticated posing trunks and a better feeling about my posing routine. My father had become interested in seeing me compete. He had started turning up at the gym now and then, and coming into the basement during my late workouts. I think he realized that I had true potential, because he started pushing me and bragging about me.

"How do I look, Dad?"

The Mr. Wagner Contest,
1971

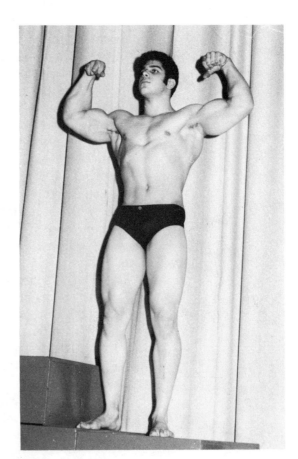

"Fantastic, Louie. I think you're going to beat everybody. You're so big."

But I didn't beat everybody. Steve Michalik won the Mr. Wagner. I came in second in the tall man's class. Still, I felt good about my showing. Steve was four or five years older than I. And I was certain I could surpass him in less than half that time. Once more my double-biceps pose brought down the house. It was a fantastic feeling to be onstage with an audience. When I walked out to accept my trophy I hit the double-biceps again just to hear the applause. All the way home I kept touching my trophy and looking at it. It was the first thing I had won. It wasn't great, but it represented a lot of what I knew was to come.

"Keep training, Louie," my father said before we got out of the car. "A year or two and you'll blow them all away."

"I'll never stop, Dad."

At the Mr. Wagner Contest I had seen a lot of bodybuilders with their girlfriends, and that made me envious. I wished I had someone to share my experiences with. But I was so big, and I was still backward about girls. I had never had a date. The one girl had stood me up and that was it. My social life was zero. I went out with my friends to bars and discos, trying to find girls, but they would see me approaching and they would either turn away, frightened by my size, or they would giggle and laugh. They seemed to be saying that I couldn't be serious about wanting to ask them for a dance. I was shy, and it didn't take much of a rebuke to turn me off. I would leave and get rid of my frustrations by going to a restaurant or drive-in and stuffing myself until I couldn't move. I would sleep it off, wake up feeling guilty, and spend all day Saturday or Sunday trying to work away those extra calories in the gym.

Ordinarily I am pretty even-tempered. Training promotes this. You take out most of your aggressions with the weights. But one day after an embarrassing rejection by a girl, I was driving home and wanted to pass a car. When I beeped my horn for the guy to move over he turned and swore at me out of his open window. I eased in front of him so he couldn't get around me and stopped my car. Pulling myself up to full height and keeping my arms flexed, I walked back to his car. He cowered away from the window, afraid I would hit him. I looked at him for a minute and said: "Don't ever call me names again. It really upsets me."

A couple of days later my mother got a call from one of her friends. She said, "Tell Louie that my son didn't mean to call him a name."

I knew who he was—a kid I had gone to school with at St. Athanasius, one of the guys who had called me Deaf Louie, but I had not recognized him because of his long hair. I wondered if he thought that was my way of getting back at him. Nothing could have been further from the truth. I never held a grudge.

My third competition that year was the AAU Mr. Teenage America. I felt myself coming closer. People were beginning to talk about me. The first thing anybody noticed, of course, was my arms. Gradually, however, the rest of my body was catching up. Like a lot of other bodybuilders just starting out, I had given all my attention to the showy parts of the upper body. You can see the same thing in early photographs of Arnold Schwarzenegger and Dave Draper. After seeing Larry Scott I blasted away at the rest of my body, especially my legs, which were really shallow, and I was making phenomenal progress. I could feel it; I was starting to see it.

It all came together, finally, at the Mr. Teenage Eastern America Contest in Asbury Park, New Jersey. I cut my weight from 225 to 218. I was training with less weight and more reps at an accelerated rate. For the first time in my life I was cut, I had definition. The contest was a clear victory for me. I knew this when I walked into the warm-up room backstage and saw how my competitors looked at me. I won the contest at that moment. I remember coming out with the lineup and stepping to the center for the compulsory poses before the judging panel, and feeling as if I were already accepting the trophy. As someone told me later, it was like seeing a Mr. Olympia contestant competing for Mr. Brooklyn.

What a great feeling it was to win! But it was like letting a shark taste a little blood. I became very hungry. I was so hungry, in fact, that I set my sights for the Mr. Teenage America and in a little over six weeks I had put on almost 10 more pounds of solid muscle.

The Mr. Teenage America was held in conjunction with the Mr. America and the Mr. World contests. There was a huge audience, and winning meant a fantastic amount of exposure. I had one title under my belt; the joy of that win was fresh in my mind, and there was no one who was going to beat me. That was my attitude that night. I was ready. This was a kind of milestone, because it was to be my last small-time contest. It was my farewell to the boys.

I could not have done better. People applauded and applauded, and I remember the announcer saying to the audience: "Can you believe this bodybuilder is only nineteen years old?" I finished my posing and received a standing ovation. I went into the winner's circle with Boyer Coe, who had won Mr. World, and Pete Caputo, who had won Mr. America. We were like kings.

With the Mr. Teenage America title my reputation took a tremendous stride forward and I was invited to give my first posing exhibition. It was set up through Julie Levine at R&J Health Club as part of a program to be given one weekend on Fire Island.

I was nervous. I packed a bag, then realized I had forgotten my oil. I put it in. I made sure I had a cassette of my posing music. It was too early to leave. I sat my mother down in the kitchen and made her watch my routine.

"What do you think, Mom? Do you think I should keep in this back shot, or is it better without it?"

The Teenage Eastern
America competition

"It looks great, Louie. But maybe it'd be just as good if you left it out. How should I know? What feels best to you?"

"You're no help, Mom. I'm asking a question. I want your advice."

"Louie, you're all worked up. My advice is just go do it. You'll be a sensation."

To get to Fire Island, I had to take a ferry from Long Island. I found myself on board with almost all women, but it was strange because they didn't shy away from me the way girls ordinarily did. They wanted to be friendly and talk. Some of them were so gorgeous. Then, about halfway to Fire Island, it suddenly hit me what was going on: These were transvestites, men dressed up as women. It was a troupe of female impersonators and their friends, guys who would be on the program with me.

That was only the beginning. Fire Island totally freaked me out. There is something deceptive about a bodybuilder as young and big as I was at that stage. I appeared to possess a maturity I was lacking. I understood almost nothing about women, let alone men who wanted to dress like women or assume a female role. I stepped off the ferry and saw men holding hands and walking around. I started to feel uneasy about my performance. All these guys were skinny. Among them, I felt like a giant. I was certain they would hate my exhibition. Everywhere I was taken by the promoter, people seemed to know who I was. These guys would come up and shake my hand and then stand back and just look at me.

The only thing I had to do to bring down the house was step out on stage. These guys screamed and screamed, and when I hit my first pose and flexed they went wild. I finished my routine. I

42

A.A.U. Teenage Mr. America. I was
nineteen years old

did an encore. Then one guy ran up out of the audience, ripped off
all his clothes, and yelled: "Lou Ferrigno, you're God. I love you."
I didn't know what to do. This guy was trying to get to me. He said
he wanted to kiss me. I was ready to jump off the stage and run for
my life when the promoters got the guy to gather up his clothes
and go back into the audience.

That was the last time I went to Fire Island.

That was also a year that marked the change of a lot of things
for me. All my life I had been frightened of my father when he was
angry. For years he had threatened me with his belt, and when I
became too old for that he came at me with his hands. He would
grab me, give me a shake, and make as if he was going to hit me. It
never occurred to me that I could ever hit him back. I never would
have, of course. Then an incident came up when I was teasing my
little sister about something and my father came in and actually
started hitting me. I turned to the side and let him pound away on
my arm and shoulder, which I kept flexed and hard. "Dad," I said,
"are you going to cut it out?" I saw that he was hurting his fists on
me, and finally he did back down.

The next time we got into an argument he didn't try to hit me.
He jumped up and shouted: "Dammit, Louie, I'm going to get my
gun." He started into the bedroom, where he kept his uniform,
and I ran for the street. I didn't think he would shoot me, but then
I hadn't thought he would hit me, either.

Still, it was as my mother insisted: "Your father is your father,
Louie. He has a temper. But it only shows how much he loves you,
how much he cares."

I knew that was true. But sometimes I did wonder. One night
he dumped a huge bowl of salad over my head and then made a

dash into his bedroom for his gun. I ran into the street with let-tuce and tomatoes all over me and vinegar and oil dripping out of my hair. Who knows what our neighbors thought.

I had become an enigma to the men at New York Sheet Metal. I was starting to slack off. Part of the problem was my training schedule. I stayed late at the gym, putting in monstrous workouts. I really needed more sleep, but I had to be on the job by seven. The guys couldn't understand why I kept it up. "Hey, Rhino, what you going to do with all those trophies—go home at night and polish them?" They called me Baby Rhino, the Brooklyn Behemoth, the Giant Killer. I used to grit my teeth and say to myself, You'll see, you'll see. I had a desire they would never understand, let alone know how it felt. I said to myself: If I have to do it forever for noth-ing, I will, because I love it.

Nobody could believe how much I ate. Even I couldn't believe I went from 220 pounds in the fall to 315 in the spring—almost 100 pounds in a few months. I ate nine meals and snacks every day. Everything in my body seemed accelerated. I did crazy things. I bent 60-penny spikes with one hand. I went behind the shop and picked up a length of railroad track. I was huge, a mon-ster. I wanted to be the first 300-pound bodybuilder. Which meant I needed to take my weight up as far as I could, then cut it down to 300.

I ate anything I could get my hands on. It didn't matter if I were hungry or not. I force-fed myself. People at the gym kept saying, "You're crazy, Louie—you can't get that big without tak-ing steroids." But I didn't want to take any drugs. For years I had seen my father come in after dealing with junkies. He would tell me how it broke his heart to go up on a rooftop or down in the cor-ner of a boiler room or in a cheap hotel room and find a fifteen- or sixteen-year-old kid with a needle in his vein. The kid would be dead, the belt still cinched around his arm, his fingers already turning black. Those images had stayed with me, and I wanted no part of drugs, any kind of drugs.

The one food I really went overboard on was tunafish. We bought Italian tuna by the case. It had a much stronger odor than regular tuna but I thought the taste was better. My father got so the smell made him sick, and he wouldn't allow me to eat it when we were together for meals. "Eat it at work, Louie. I don't care if you have a hundred tuna sandwiches at work, but not when you're having dinner with me." Late at night when I came home from the gym I used to open a can and just stand in the kitchen and eat it with a fork. My father couldn't even stand that. He would open his bedroom door and shout: "Go down in the base-ment and eat your tuna!" The smell of tuna would actually wake him up.

One night, after what must have been a nerve-wracking day for my father, I had just finished a can of tuna when I heard him come storming out of the bedroom. I ran into my own room, got under the covers, and pretended to be asleep. My father was really fuming and I was afraid he had his police revolver, but I didn't dare peek to see for sure. He left finally, and I started laughing so hard the bed shook. Then I heard him coming back. I thought he must have heard me. I buried my face in the pillow. He stopped and poured a whole can of oil and tuna under my bed so I would be forced to smell it all night and then tossed the empty can on my pillow.

I could laugh about some of my father's antics, but he did one thing that seriously upset me. After I had won the Mr. Teenage Eastern America, Joe Weider, the publisher of *Muscle Builder Magazine*, wrote to ask if I would be interested in coming to California. In that first letter he said, "Arnold Schwarzenegger, who is an expert bodybuilder, will be glad to work with you and teach you all the latest techniques in bodybuilding."

I was really happy with that letter. My one big dream had been to go to California, to the sunshine and the beach where Arnold and Ken Waller and Frank Zane and the other great bodybuilders worked out in the best gyms. But to have Arnold personally interested in helping me was more than I could ever have hoped for. I couldn't wait for my father to see the letter. It meant Joe Weider considered me prime championship material.

My father looked at the letter and shook his head. "No, Louie, I don't think you should do this. California's three thousand miles away. You're too young. You've never been away from home."

I argued that I had to leave sometime.

"What will they give you?" he wanted to know. "A pittance?"

"I don't know that yet, Dad. I don't care."

"I pulled some strings to get you the job you've got. You're making good money, son. I don't see how you can afford to quit."

That sent me to the gym to work off the biggest depression I'd had since winning the title.

Joe Weider was persistent. At the next contest in New York, where I was competing for Mr. America, he talked to me backstage. "Look at that arm on Arnold Schwarzenegger, Lou. Wouldn't you love to have an arm like that? You should come to California and train. After three months you would look fantastic. You could pack on twenty pounds of muscle. You could win any contest."

My father still insisted Joe wasn't offering enough to make it worth my while. It's true there wasn't a lot of money in it, but I said I could get along.

"No, Louie, you're better off working at New York Sheet Metal."

That was the point at which I told myself there was no opposition big enough to stop me. There was nothing I could not overcome. If it was impossible to go to California I would continue to train on my own. I decided then and there that the time had come to stop piddling around, that I was going to move into the professional ranks and win Mr. America.

Most people have never understood my relationship with my father. Numerous times I was told I was crazy to listen to him, that he was selfish or jealous, that he was ruining my life. All they knew, of course, was how it appeared from the outside. Between my father and me it was a different story.

For two very good reasons, my father was concerned about my welfare and my future. My hearing problem made many types of employment difficult or impossible—which he felt he had solved with the sheet metal job. Then too, he was concerned about his ability to continue to help me if I should need it.

This particular fear was very real. My grandfather, Lou Ferrigno, had died from Hodgkin's disease—cancer of the lymph glands—which has often proved to be hereditary. My father, and I too, of course, had to consider our own chances of contracting the disease. And indeed five years after the death of my grandfather, as my father was shaving one morning (it happened to be his thirty-seventh birthday), he felt an unusual lump on his neck. A biopsy showed it was Hodgkin's disease. He underwent local radiation treatments and it seemed to be stopped.

Because I was nine years old at the time, no one explained any of this to me then. I was told only that my father was going into the hospital for a small operation. My father showed me the lump and that was all. I didn't realize his doctor had warned him that at the most he had two years to live, a terrible judgment that luckily turned out to be false.

Eight years later he found another lump in the same area. He went to the hospital to have it checked. I remember when he came home from that visit. They had cut a slit in the top of each foot and injected a dye into his veins. The dye could be seen on the X-ray and indicated that he had enlarged lymph nodes. He showed me the cuts in his feet and talked to me about the disease and what the doctors had said to him. He had two choices: surgery, which would probably be extensive this time, or radiation, also extensive. Both the surgeon and the radiologist had argued their cases. Given my father's personality it is understandable that he went with the surgeon's view. "Don't leave any cinders behind, Mr. Ferrigno," the surgeon had said. "Cut it out and have done with it." That was the kind of talk my father could understand.

I went to see him after the operation. He was propped up in the hospital bed. They had taken almost all of the muscle out of one side of his neck and chest, and there were still clamps on him to keep the wounds closed. It was very frightening. I started to say something, then quit. "Louie," he said, "I don't want you to think about me. I'll get through this. Concentrate on your work. Help your mother."

To make matters worse, when he was healing up and almost ready to come home, his doctors gathered around his bed one morning and said they strongly recommended that he also undergo radiation treatment. Failure to do it might cost him his life.

My father tried to explain what they did. "It's like frying an egg," he said. "They radiate you on your back one day and then they turn you over the next day and do your front."

I went with my mother once to pick him up after a radiation. He looked terrible. And he vomited all the time we were driving home. It was the last time I asked to go.

The disease was stopped once more. Seeing my father go through the surgery and the treatments gave me a better understanding of the pressures on him; it strengthened my respect for him and his attitude about my life and my security, although it did not dampen my desire to be a great bodybuilder.

Professional contest training is a full-time job—if for no other reason than the fact that most of your serious competitors are usually working out around the clock. This includes hard training twice a day, resting in between, taking time to eat right, sleeping properly, and maintaining a perfect tan. This put me at a slight disadvantage when I decided to go after the Mr. America title. I was still a full-time sheet-metal worker; nothing I said could convince my father that it would be wise to quit work and devote all my energy and time to working out. "For what, Louie? For another trophy?"

"Guys make money in bodybuilding, Dad."

"What guys?"

"Look at Arnold. Arnold makes thousands of dollars a year."

"Arnold and who else?" he asked. "No one. The rest of them get chickenfeed. Arnold's a big star."

"I'm going to be a star, Dad. I'm going to be a superstar."

"Meanwhile, you're not even twenty-one, Louie. You haven't made a dime from bodybuilding. You don't have the slightest idea what you're talking about."

The pressure I put on myself that year was tremendous. Besides working and eating, the only things I did were training and sleeping. Maybe I should have gone to California in spite of my father—the idea occurred to me many times over the next few months—but I could not bring myself to go against his wishes.

I continued to grow. I blew up so big that nobody could walk past me without doing a double-take. I had 22½-inch arms, a chest almost five feet around; I stood six feet five and weighed nearly 300 pounds. Total strangers would stop me on the street and say, "God, you're big." At the gym I was a focal point. I thrived on that attention, even though I knew that it was potentially dangerous to my continued progress. I needed competition. I have always fed on competition. I would have made even greater progress if I had been in California, where I would have had to put up a struggle to be the center of attention.

Guys at the gym kept coming over and telling me I had the title. More than anything I wanted to believe that, but I knew I had faults, serious faults. For one thing, I needed more back and greater depth in my legs. My continuous eating had thickened my waist, and I was frantically chiseling away at it. There was a layer of fat under my skin that I wanted to lose, that I *had* to lose if I expected to get anyplace in the Mr. America.

Six weeks before the competition I cut my diet drastically and started to burn off the fat. I knew very little about the fine points of dieting and almost nothing about supplements—more "secrets" Joe Weider had promised to enlighten me about in California. I cut sugar from my diet and kept up my intake of protein, which was nearly the full extent of my knowledge of nutrition.

My father had become more involved. In the beginning, before I really knew anything about the dedication it took to be a winner, we had driven hundreds of miles to small competitions, lost, and come home to commiserate and lick our wounds. My father was not with me the same way he would be later during my training for the Mr. Olympia in South Africa and the simultaneous filming of *Pumping Iron*, but we talked together every day. This was usually at the dinner table. We had always been a close family, and we spent this time talking about bodybuilding. My mother had never gone to a contest; I don't know why but she always backed down at the last moment. Still, she joined in our dinner table talk and she wanted to help. "What shall I cook, Louie? What would be best for you?"

As the competition came closer, the pitch of excitement at the dinner table rose. My posing routine took up more and more of the discussion. I can remember that even after eating I would jump up and try a shot on them.

"Confidence, Louie," my father would say. "That's the secret. Look confident."

"I *am* confident."

"Then show it, dammit!"

My father never really praised me. He pushed me, criticized me, and encouraged me, but he never gave me praise. Years later, he said, "I was raising a family, not running a popularity contest. I thought if I told you you looked good you'd let down in your training. If I kept harping on your weak points you would train harder than ever."

Which was only part of the truth. When he told me that he had mellowed a lot. But he was from a different generation, and he had no idea how to temper his criticism with praise, to soften the blow, to make it easier on me.

Sometimes after he made a negative comment I would stomp away from the dinner table. But I would find myself downstairs, checking my body in the mirror, trying to figure out what to do.

Two weeks more, I said to myself the day before the Mr. America. I could see it—plain as day: I needed exactly two more weeks to achieve the finish I needed. I was so conscious of that last remaining little bit of fat that I could feel it when I flexed.

I had made two serious mistakes: I had bulked up too much and then tried to lose too much weight too fast. I had gone from 315 to 259 pounds in barely six and a half months. Through crash dieting I had lost too much muscle size and mass and failed even to achieve the definition I wanted.

I saw the guys from the California gyms the instant I walked through the backstage door. They had heard about me, and they were waiting to check me out.

It was a confusing night for me. Sometime during my pumping up backstage my hearing aid quit working. For a few years I had been wearing a style of hearing aid that fit behind my ear. I slipped into the toilet stall, took it off, and fiddled with it. There was nothing I could do; the battery was dead. I was ashamed to let my competitors know I wore the thing. My father had already gone down into the audience. It was one of those disastrous moments I had feared—like the time I was lost in the woods. I was no less lost that night. All the identifiable sounds drifted away. Only by looking hard at a person's mouth could I get any idea of what he was trying to tell me. People must have thought I was stoned or stupid. I saw those looks when they kept repeating that it was time to get in place, time to get in place. Finally, I found a friend from the gym and told him I needed someone to tell me when they called my name.

In retrospect, the events of that evening are funny. But at the time they were not. My friend gave me a shove when the announcer said my name and I walked onstage. Flashbulbs started going off, and I could see people applauding. However, as soon as the lights went down on the audience I couldn't tell what was happening. Because I couldn't hear my music I started posing and just hoped for the best. I completed my routine, which ran less than three minutes. I didn't hear much applause, and the lights stayed down. I figured that I'd blown it, that the audience hadn't liked me that much. But the opposite was true—they were clapping and clapping and trying to get me back. The next day at the gym there was a big joke about it: The audience was yelling more, more, and Big Lou just walked off the stage.

From that night on, I went nowhere without a whole pack of batteries. Even now, it is a major concern. I make sure my wife, Carla, has some fresh batteries in her purse in addition to the ones I carry.

I did not win that first Mr. America Contest. Bill Grant won the title and I came in second. I was disappointed and my family was disappointed. However, the prize for the first three winners was a chance to compete in the NABB Mr. Universe Contest in London the next week, all expenses paid. And I was being sent. I got some satisfaction from the trip, because with new judges in another country I did beat Bill Grant. I came in fourth place for the Mr. U. Seeing British bodybuilders was an eye opener for me. They were noted for their definition, their legs, and their abdominals—three areas where I was still in trouble.

England was my first foreign country. I went out to do some sightseeing. However, once I was on the street, I had the feeling it was England that had come to see me and not I who was the tourist. People stared. When I stopped one woman to ask which bus I should take to Hyde Park, she said, "Oh my God!" and turned and ran away.

Back in New York, I decided I was through bulking up. I had learned my lesson. It was time to be more sensible and concentrate on building muscle instead of mass. For most of the year I planned to maintain my body at about 75 percent perfect contest shape, then I would bomb it with hard, hard work and go right to the top. I allowed myself more time before the Mr. America competition to cut down. It was not as it had been the year before when I could feel that extra bit of fat. On the final day I was ready to win.

I weighed 282 pounds. When I first walked onstage it was as if the people had seen King Kong. They went absolutely bananas. No matter how confident I felt, I couldn't help being nervous. At a big contest I had a habit of coming out on the stage too fast, hitting my first pose almost as soon as I stepped up on the dais, then speeding through the rest of the routine as quickly as possible. Backstage before the contest, my father was coaching me. "God, you're big, Louie—it's like oiling up an elephant." Then he started harping on how I should slow down when I posed, be more deliberate, let people see me and be knocked out by my size. During the prejudging, with its small audience, he had sat close enough so I could see him and then he had signaled me on how long to hold a pose before going into the next one. But he could not do that at night during the regular performance. So before the show, he kept saying, "Don't hurry into it, Louie. Step up on the platform, then pause a second before you throw your double-arm. Count it out."

That night, I did go out without hurrying. I stepped up on the dais, pulled myself to full height, and waited. The place got silent. Someone told me later that after about fifteen seconds they could hear my father whispering: "That's enough, Louie, that's enough."

When I did throw my first double-biceps pose, it was devastating. People screamed and cried out.

I won that Mr. America by a wide margin.

It was a great night for me. I loved the idea of winning, I loved the crowd, everything. But the triumphant feeling of satisfaction

Mr. America, 1973

and fulfillment was short-lived. It seemed that even as I was reaching out to accept the trophy and knew I was being given the title of Mr. America, which was something I had whispered to myself for years, my mind was already on something else: the Mr. Olympia. If I had been hungry in the past, I was starved now.

The prize for winning Mr. America was a trip to Geneva, Switzerland, to compete in the Mr. Universe contest. Even backstage after I'd won the America people started giving me advice about the Universe—most of it negative. "I doubt if you can win this year, Louie," one bodybuilder said, shaking his head. "You need another year of hard training," said a second. "You're not polished enough, not refined," observed a third. "You'll be going out against Ken Waller and Mike Katz." And so on. As usual, I said nothing—but inside I resolved to show them. I was good enough to win.

I had six weeks before I had to be in Switzerland. I told my father I was taking the time off work so I could devote my whole day to training. I was taking a chance, because at that time there had been a slowdown in the sheet-metal industry and they were laying men off right and left. My father knew about the layoffs, but he saw that I meant to do it. He did a funny turnaround. Instead of really arguing with me, he said: "All right. This is an opportunity for you to win. If you can't do it this year you'll never do it." Seeing me win the Mr. America had meant as much to my father as it had to me, and maybe even more. It had made him a believer, and he became my staunchest supporter.

He could not believe I was training even harder than before. "Is it good to train this hard?" he wanted to know. "Can't you get hurt?"

"I've got to," I told him. "I'm going to win."

That was the spirit I took into the final weeks of training. The whole emphasis of my workouts was to shape and refine the muscle mass I had. I used every polishing technique I knew: I began doing Lunges instead of Squats; I added Cable Pulls and tried different dumbbell positions to reach the hard-to-get-at areas of a muscle. I did not waste a minute of any day. I knew exactly what I lacked and the precise exercise or variation on an exercise to fit my needs.

I went on a strict diet—tuna, meat, water. I ate one piece of fruit a day. I asked my mother to help me. She was relentless. If I even looked at pasta, she pulled the plate farther away and said, "No, Louie. That's not for you." I had never in my life been so hungry. About one in the morning when I felt a gnawing in my stomach I would sneak into the kitchen and barely open the refrigerator just enough so I could get my hand in and not let out too much light. Then I would hear my mother's voice:

"Louie, do you want to win that contest?"

"Yes, Ma, I want to win."

I would drink a glass of water and go back to bed.

52

My father and me

One week before the Geneva contest I had a posing exhibition to do with Ken Waller in Belgium. When I arrived at the airport on my way to Europe, Ken was in the terminal waiting for his connecting flight. He was with a reporter, doing an interview for a magazine. The woman came over to me after they finished, asked me a few questions, then told me Ken had said I was making a big mistake by competing. I asked why he had said that. Because they're going to wipe you out, she said. I just laughed. "He doesn't know how good I look."

In Belgium, Ken Waller and I trained in the same gym for a couple of days before the exhibition. I was still working on keeping all the water sweated out of my system, so I wore heavy sweat clothes. Ken could tell nothing about my condition, and it was beginning to bother him. The second day he walked over to me. "Big Lou," he said, "let's see how you look."

I took off my sweatshirt and hit a pose. I was down to 256 pounds and I had razor-sharp definition. I was in the best shape of my whole life. Ken looked at me and went all quiet; his face fell as if he were numb. "Ken," I said, "you okay?"

"Sure," he said. But he sat down. "You look great, Lou." The next day he wrote a card to Arnold Schwarzenegger: *Arnold, watch this kid in two years.*

One big advantage the California bodybuilders had was being able to have a decent tan, which makes a great deal of difference to your look in competition. New York has never been noted for its unlimited sunshine, and I had to try everything to catch enough sun to get brown. It became a concern of my whole family. One day my father saw a refrigerator box someone had thrown out on the street. A couple of blocks later he was struck with an idea of how he could use it. He drove back, loaded it on top of the VW, and brought it home. He and my mother lined the inside of it with aluminum foil. We took it to the roof and I spent every spare hour I had lying in that foil-lined box. That had helped me prepare for the Mr. America Contest; however, during the two weeks before I left for Switzerland there hadn't been a single hour of continuous sun in New York.

At various times I had experimented with most of the tanning formulas on the market and found I had the most success with a Helena Rubinstein product called Quick Tan. After all my contests and exhibitions, my mother had become expert at applying it; in fact, once she finished no one could tell it wasn't the real thing. People thought I had just returned from a week in Florida.

In Belgium I had used up my supply of Quick Tan. I was able to buy a tube of Braggi in Geneva, but I had never used that brand. It was no time to be experimenting. Contest rules stated it was illegal to appear with an artificial tan. I waited until late the night before the beginning of the competition to keep from getting caught by a contest official. Oscar State, the chief judge, had declared they might test to see if anyone had used tanning lotion.

But this seemed a pretty empty threat; I knew how hurried and hectic things became on the day of a contest and decided to take my chances. I convinced one of the Italian competitors to help me. Since he spoke no English I demonstrated on one leg what I needed to have him do.

I don't know what happened. The Italian guy started to smear on the Braggi and it didn't look right. He tried to fix it, but the more he worked the worse it got. It began to streak and go blotchy until I looked like a rainbow. The Italian glanced up at me, tried to speak, then just shrugged. I went out of my mind. I woke up a couple of guys I knew. I didn't know what to do. I was in tears. I couldn't show up like that. I was afraid I had blown the whole contest.

"Take it easy, Louie," one friend said. They shoved me in the shower and made me scrub off all the tanning lotion. When I was dry they started tanning my whole body. The process took three hours, but when they were finished every area of skin was perfect.

I won the Mr. Universe, the one all the bodybuilders said I couldn't win. It was like getting two titles; I was twenty-one, the youngest person ever to win the IFBB Mr. Universe, and I won by unanimous decision. The bodybuilders who were there and had seen me in the Mr. America could not believe the changes I had made in six weeks. I had trimmed off 26 pounds and still kept most of my size, a phenomenal feat.

When I called Brooklyn that night after the competition it was still afternoon and my father was in the back part of the house getting ready to start plastering a closet. My brother answered the phone upstairs. I heard him drop the receiver and go racing downstairs screaming that I had won. Then he got back on the upstairs phone.

"Where's Dad?" I asked. "I want to talk to him."

"Oh, man, Louie. He just sat down in a corner and started to cry into a towel."

When my father got to the phone he was still sobbing. My whole family was overwhelmed. After I hung up they talked and cried together. It was almost an hour later that my father remembered he had been plastering. He ran back to the closet. Too late. The plaster had hardened in the wheelbarrow and he had to chip it out with a hammer.

I was flying high—Mr. America and Mr. Universe within a few weeks. I felt I was on top of the world. *ABC Wide World of Sports* covered the show in Switzerland, and afterward they did an interview with me. I thought it was great. Here was a room full of lights and cameras and I was talking with a man I'd seen many times on network television. It was my first taste of being a star, the feeling I had longed for since seeing Arnold for the first time and trying to imagine what it would be like to be famous.

I spent a few days traveling in Italy—mostly eating, trying to make up for the weeks and weeks of an almost straight high-protein diet. During the time I traveled and relaxed I daydreamed

Winning the Mr. Universe competition

about the *Wide World of Sports* program, how it would be put together, how my interview would be cut in with the action and drama of the contest. The producer had been enthusiastic about the fact that I was so young, so big, so finished.

However, when I stepped off the plane my father informed me that the interview would not be included in the show. They had shortened it and used only footage of the contest.

I felt as if I'd been hit with a hammer. "Why not, Dad?"

"They don't want it to hurt you, son."

"What do you mean—*hurt* me?"

"Nobody could understand what you were saying. I went to the studio in Manhattan and saw it, Louie. They're right."

It was like walking into a dark tunnel. Perhaps depression hits me harder than a lot of people because I rarely experience it, but when it does come it's very difficult for me to handle. I had spent

Posing in Italy

almost fifteen years working on my speech, on understanding and trying to be understood. Still, that had not been enough to allow me to communicate the joy of my achievements to a television audience. My world collapsed. The only time I seemed able to regain a sense of myself was in the gym.

Joe Weider contacted me and offered me a contract to come to California. For some reason, I had felt my success in the America and Universe contests would open my father's eyes. But again he said no, don't do it, Louie. There wasn't enough money. He said they would get me out there and take advantage of me. That only made me feel worse.

To further complicate matters, my job at New York Sheet Metal was filled and my boss would not take me back. I was living at home, depressed, with almost no income, and my father was upset because I had lost my job. Up to that time I suppose I had limited myself to merely being understood on a basic level, and then I had retreated into the comfort of my basement gym. Now bodybuilding had demanded more than I was prepared to give. I looked at this as a personal failure: I had set my goals too low, I had not been hard enough on myself.

Bodybuilding had been my greatest teacher. Through it I had learned to solve problems. If my legs seemed to have less development than my arms I sought the exercises that benefited the legs and then bombarded them with work and brought them to the condition I wanted. My main problem at that time was my speech impediment, and I had to conquer that in order to reach the place I wanted to be, and I had to conquer my fear of people's knowing I wore a hearing aid. Once I had made this decision to overcome the problem I felt an immediate surge of energy.

I began by going to a dentist and having my front teeth fixed to get rid of the space between them, which helped give clarity to my *s* sounds. From that point on it would take more than a couple of hours in the dentist chair. And it went deeper than the palate. I was a prisoner of the protective shell I had built around me; I realized this and wanted to break out.

Through the sheet-metal union I discovered that there was a good possibility of work in Columbus, Ohio. I went to Ohio. I hadn't worked for some time and arrived with only $40 in my pocket. I didn't mind that because the feeling of finally getting out on my own was worth it.

I rented a room at the YMCA for a week, then I found my own apartment. I made friends with some of the young guys at the sheet-metal shop where I worked and gradually started finding my way out of the depression that had hit me upon my return from Europe.

The *Wide World of Sports* show was finally aired. Knowing my interview had been cut, I could barely bring myself to sit in front of my set, but the show was better than I had imagined it would be, and it had an incredible effect. Ordinary people who knew nothing about bodybuilding began recognizing me on the street, and that was exactly what I needed to push me back onto course. I began to train again at Ohio State University. The owner of Jack Bowman's Steak House hired me to be a weekend host. In many ways this extra job was the best thing I could have done, as it forced me to be out in public, to see and talk to different people. I can't believe how uptight I was in the beginning. When the first couple came in I actually began to sweat. I was worried about getting them to the right table, about understanding what they said.

Jack Bowman became my personal friend. I'll never forget how good he was to me and how much he put up with. His son was interested in working out with weights. I started him on a program, and we occasionally trained together at the university gym.

I had begun to talk to the girls who worked in the steak house. At first, they moved away from me, as girls always had, but gradually they grew accustomed to my size. They had seen me on TV. It was different than it had been going to discos and singles bars with my friends. I wanted to go out and couldn't because I was still afraid to ask a girl and I didn't want another rejection. Then one of the girls completed the question for me: Why didn't we go to a movie? I couldn't believe it. It was my first date. I was twenty-one.

I started dating one girl on a steady basis. Her name was Kay, and she seemed to satisfy something in my life that I had not known I needed. In a short time, we became very close. I found I could talk to her about inner feelings I had never shared with anyone else. The idea of a relationship and the world it opened up was as astonishing to me as it was new. It was like getting a million dollars every day.

Any trace of depression that lingered from the aftermath of the Mr. Universe Contest was wiped out by this surge of happiness. I felt rejuvenated and full of a new energy. I continued to work at the sheet-metal shop and the restaurant, to train in the gym and try to get myself back in shape. Kay helped a great deal. I learned from her how valuable it was to have someone who was solid, who had her head screwed on right. As a result I never took up with bodybuilding groupies or girls who were cheap.

Kay was, I think, somewhat bewildered by me. I talked about bodybuilding all the time, about contests and other competitors, but mostly I talked about myself and how I was methodically working to become the biggest, greatest bodybuilder in the world. By listening and giving me her time she was fulfilling one of the fantasies that had been with me since I had begun to compete and win: to have a woman who would share my bodybuilding triumphs, who would take an interest in it and want to be a part of it.

My new social life did not prevent me from getting back into a strict workout schedule. I trained six days a week and took only Sunday off.

On my own in Ohio

Toning up in Brooklyn

Three months before the next Mr. Universe Contest I quit work and returned to New York for my final concentrated period of training. After being on my own, I hated moving back into the old house on 5th Street. It was harder for me to leave Ohio because of Kay, but we kept in touch by phone. My folks saw how serious I was and started to question me. Who was this girl? What did she look like? What did she do? Actually, I was afraid to tell them very much because I knew they would not approve.

One weekend Kay came to visit me in New York. My father and mother began asking her the same questions. When they found out she was divorced, that she had a child, they had a fit. It made her nervous being around my folks, and her whole attitude toward me changed. Finally she said she wanted to break up. She said I was too young, too immature, for her; I wasn't the kind of man she wanted.

I was heartbroken. This had been my first love, and it had been important to me. Kay had taught me about the richness of being able to share my fantasies and dreams with another person, and I didn't want to believe it was over. What kept me going, kept me from sliding back into my depression, was my personal belief that once I got through this contest and went back to Ohio everything would be okay again.

Sometime during the turmoil of that period I was invited to a party at the Olympia Health Club. Dennis Tinerinno and a few other of the best bodybuilders were there. One attraction that evening was a man who claimed to be the world's champion pinch-grip lifter. He would pinch steel plates between his thumb and forefinger and lift them off the floor. He claimed he could do 90 pounds that way. He came on with this long, cocky rap about how difficult it was and all the famous places he had performed this feat. He got the plates together, strained and strained, and gradually lifted the 90 pounds a few inches off the floor before they slipped from his fingers. Then he challenged the audience, saying he knew we were so-called strongmen, but just how strong were we? Come on, who wanted to prove his superior strength.

I had been thinking I could do it, and finally I volunteered. I said, "How am I supposed to hold it? Like this?" I pinched the two 45-pound plates together and lifted them to my waist and held them. That guy's face fell a foot. I think I was as amazed as he was—though not as disappointed. Everybody cheered: "Big Lou! Come on, more!"

I went up to 120 pounds. I've always wondered if the guy continued going around claiming to be the pinch-grip champion of the world.

My interest in nutrition had reached a point where I was trying to find out as much as I could on a scientific level. Through Julie Levine at the gym I heard there would be a seminar on nutrition for the bodybuilder given by a man named Bill Drake, who was well-known in bodybuilding circles. He had worked out himself and had developed a line of products for bodybuilders. One of Bill Drake's examples of a bodybuilder who used supplements to great advantage was his friend Arnold Schwarzenegger. During his seminar, Bill said, "Arnold has the largest measurements of any bodybuilder."

"Bullshit," I called out.

Drake stopped his lecture. "What?"

"I said, '*Bullshit.*' I'm bigger than Arnold."

Bill wouldn't believe it.

"Show him, Lou," the bodybuilders shouted.

I stood up and hit a few poses.

Bill still wouldn't believe it. He was like a lot of people in whose minds Arnold was a god. Nobody could be bigger than Arnold, nobody could do anything better. Not even the tape measure was proof enough for them—or Bill.

I do not know if Bill ever really believed I was bigger, but we did become friends and he answered a lot of questions I had about nutrition. He too urged me to come to the West Coast, but he said I needed to have my head on straight and not be like a lot of bodybuilders who were mixed up and into the drug scene.

In June or July I had a phone call from Arnold Schwarzenegger asking if I would come to California and guest-pose for an

With Joe Weider in California

exhibition he was producing. He had invited nine different Mr. Universe winners. I accepted and flew to L.A. It was my first trip to California. I couldn't wait to get on the ground and see the sunshine and the beach.

California was as magical as I had been led to believe. I saw why the bodybuilders had made it their mecca. A lot of people say it's laid-back, and maybe in general it is, but in the gyms there was an energy I had never seen. The beach and the sea air had an unbelievable effect on me, and I wanted more than ever to train there. I got so excited that instead of simply guest-posing I entered Arnold's contest, the Mr. International, and won it.

That year, I waited until the day before the Mr. Universe Contest to fly to Italy. I always liked to train right up to the last minute, fly in, and win. My father and mother had gone over ahead of me to visit my father's relatives in Amalfi, which is in the countryside near Naples. They were going to Verona from there. My father called the promoter, Franco Fassi, to ask him to pick me up in Milano, a four-hour drive from Verona. He said, "My son will be arriving from the United States. Could you meet his plane?"

"He should have come with the group."

"That was impossible," my father explained. "He was training."

"Then he'll have to find his own way here."

"Could you get that message to him?"

"Yes. All right. What's his name?"

"Lou Ferrigno."

"Lou Ferrigno! Why didn't you say it was Lou Ferrigno? Of course we'll pick him up. I'll send my brother with the Mercedes."

When I heard that, I knew I had come a long way up the ladder and was starting to find the recognition I had hoped for years to gain. It was a star's treatment and let me know how close I was to realizing my dream.

Bodybuilding contests are ordinarily divided into two segments. The first is the prejudging, at which there is a limited audience of contestants, press, VIPs, and family, and the second is the ceremony for awarding the prizes. Most serious decisions are made during prejudging, but it is possible for judges to make changes during the final ceremony. The prejudging is a strict affair, during which no applause or comments from the audience are allowed.

In Verona, the chief judge, Dennis Starlander, made the customary announcement of those rules, and the contest began. When Paul Grant, from Wales, slipped out and threw his first compulsory pose, the audience started to applaud. Starlander shushed the audience. His voice echoing in the hall, he said he would permit no further applause or interruption or he would clear the hall. The place got quiet as a church.

My name was called. I walked to the center of the stage, directly in front of the judges' table, hesitated, and then struck a

61

double-arm pose. The spectators went wild. Everyone applauded; even the photographers put down their cameras and clapped. The chief judge just threw up his arms, seeing there was nothing he could do about it. And there was no doubt in my mind that at that moment I had won my second Mr. Universe.

Waiting was never my game. I was never good at it. My goals were always geared to going for the top. I could have gone on winning the Mr. Universe for years, but there was one more step in the sport, the Mr. Olympia. I had to take it.

When I announced my intentions of competing for the Mr. Olympia title at Madison Square Garden the following week, everyone advised me not to do it. Serge Nubret said, "Don't enter, Louie. Give it time. You're not mature enough yet." My father pleaded with me, "Wait until there's no question. Wait until you can walk in there and take it."

I thought I could win, and I was thoroughly convinced I was ready. I was hot from winning my second Universe and now I wanted to take the big one.

I felt secure about winning. I knew Arnold Schwarzenegger was my only competition. I was confident I could beat everyone else, and in my mind I minimized even Arnold's amazing assets. I walked into Madison Square Garden with my mind fixed on coming out with the Olympia.

When I first saw Arnold he looked a little heavy, and that made me feel good. But Arnold is very deceptive. Relaxed, his body goes down unbelievably. And when we were downstairs pumping up I realized how mistaken I'd been. It seemed he would never stop getting bigger and bigger. Plus, he had that extra edge of coming in right on time. I had been in perfect shape for the Universe, but one additional week on the same rigid diet had left me too gaunt and too tired for the rigorous strain of that competition.

After the fanfare of winning in Italy, second place in the Olympia was a blow to my ego. I started sinking again. Joe Weider offered me another contract. "You look fantastic, Lou. You need to come to California for some polishing." I wanted to go but once more my father shook his head. It was the same old story; he felt Joe was not willing to pay the money I was worth. "Go back to sheet-metal work," he said. I argued that I should go to California and establish myself. It was time. "No, Louie," my father said. "Listen to me. I know what I'm talking about."

I returned to Ohio. My relationship with Kay was finished, and I saw that nothing would be the same. I felt a kind of emptiness all that winter. Ohio was cold and bleak. Something had gone wrong with my sense of direction, my goals. I knew one thing more strongly than ever: I did not want to keep working in sheet metal.

I thought about California every day. I began to resent my father's advice that I go back to Ohio and to regret that I had not made my own decision.

Three months prior to the 1975 Mr. Olympia Contest, I was approached by George Butler and Charles Gaines about being in the film *Pumping Iron*. They asked if I would go back to New York and train for the contest, which was to be held in Pretoria, South Africa. They wanted permission to bring the *Pumping Iron* crew into my home and the gym periodically to film me. I had always wanted to be in films, and I liked the idea for *Pumping Iron,* so I accepted their offer. I decided I would work hard at coming in as big as I could.

Pumping Iron was my first experience of being around a motion-picture crew and watching a film take shape; but that taste of working in front of the camera was enough to convince me that I loved the feeling of being there. And although I was not certain how I was going to do it, I was convinced that someday I was going to get into the business.

Going into the final weeks before the Olympia, I put in two long, grueling sessions at the gym each day. Again I felt I had made a mistake by bulking up too long and there would not be time enough to achieve the definition I wanted. I was definitely behind Arnold, who had been training all year. Bodybuilding was his work. It was what he did. I repeated that again and again to make myself train harder and harder. To keep everything as fresh as possible I trained in two gyms—R&J and a community health club in Queens. The officials of the club gave me a key and said to use it anytime I wanted. I went in the morning from four to eight in order to keep from being bothered by any of the members.

The first day was a disaster. My father had agreed to be with me for every workout. It was a side of our relationship George wanted to exploit in the film. We went to the health club at five in the morning, and I began the first session with Dumbbell Curls. I was using 80-pound dumbbells, and after a warm-up set I pushed myself right up to the point of pain. I screamed my way through the last couple of reps, then dropped the dumbbells to the floor. The whole building shook. Someone started hammering on the walls. "Cut it out in there!"

"Louie," Dad said, "you gotta be more quiet."

"Dad, I've got to get my workout."

About the time I moved to the bench press and started really grinding out heavy reps, someone began to pound on the door. "Open up in there—it's the police!"

My father showed the cops his badge and promised we would be quiet. They warned him they wanted no more trouble and left. He explained to me what the problem was, that I had to hold down the noise. I said I'd try not to scream, but I sometimes had to drop the weights because my strength was gone.

"Just nod your head, Louie—I'll take them from you."

I never saw my father work so hard. I kept him busy bringing weights from the racks and taking them from me when I finished a set. After a few hours of sweating, the water pouring down his face, he was as tired as I was.

In South Africa on one of the last days before the Mr. Olympia Contest I went with the rest of the bodybuilders to a national game farm where a photographer had arranged to photograph me with a cheetah. I stripped down to blue posing trunks, and my father oiled me up and took me to the area where they wanted to shoot. It was at least 115 degrees, the sun beating down. The trainer yanked and yanked at the leash on this cheetah, trying to pull him toward me, but the animal kept fighting the collar.

"You sure he's tame?" I asked.

"Nothing to worry about," the trainer assured me.

The cheetah started licking oil from my leg

I wasn't convinced. The animal rolled his eyes at me and growled as the trainer dragged him close. I froze up until I was as stiff as a statue.

"Do a twisted back shot," my father said.

I turned, flexing, showing off the pose, but my heart wasn't in it. I kept wondering what the cheetah was doing. Then I felt something touch my leg. I looked down and saw the cheetah licking the oil off my skin.

"Okay, Louie," my father called out, "the most muscular pose."

When I started to crouch into the pose, the cheetah must have thought I was going to pounce on him, because he bared his fangs. I couldn't think of anything to do. I knew I shouldn't run. So I fell over backward, and the trainer grabbed the cat.

Later, I was told that someone had made a mistake. It was the wrong cheetah—it had mistakenly been put in the cage with the tame one. I could have been killed.

As soon as the filming was finished on *Pumping Iron,* I flew to Florida, where I'd been asked to participate in the Superstars. I looked at it as my opportunity to disprove on national television the unfortunate myth that bodybuilders are muscle-bound freaks. It has always been my belief that people are more often "muscle-bound" if they are either weak or not in control of their muscles. To prove my point I trimmed off 50 pounds in six weeks; I went from 275 down to 224. I changed my entire exercise routine. I cut down the amount of weight I lifted; I rode a bike fifteen or twenty miles a day. I ran. I rowed a boat. I hit baseballs. I bowled. I kept my calorie intake at about 1,000, which meant I was hungry all the time. But determination and the knowledge of what was at stake made me refrain from eating.

I think one thing that helped me stay in this kind of training was my dread of going back to work in a sheet-metal shop. I kept hoping that after the Superstars I would find one more way to avoid ever doing that kind of work again. I did well in the Superstars, and out of it came an offer to play professional football— which was strange, because I had never played football very much in school. Maybe for that reason I didn't really get into the game. Early in the training period I was injured, and instead of allowing myself to be carried into the season on the injured reserve list, I quit.

Back in Brooklyn I told my father: "There's one more thing I want to do, Dad, and that's go to California and train. I'm going to do that, no matter what."

Finally, after all the offers we had turned down, he said, "Okay, Louie. I can see there's no way to stop you this time."

5

I suppose nobody is ever quite prepared for California. I had been in Los Angeles briefly to pose and compete in the Mr. International Contest. My memories of that trip were only positive and perhaps for that reason largely distorted. I flew out the second time to guest-pose in the Gold Classic, a competition promoted by Ken Sprague, the owner of the legendary Gold's Gym.

After *Pumping Iron* I had not gone back to sheet-metal work, which made things tough financially and put a strain on my relationship with my father. I arrived in Los Angeles with $100, which I spent almost before I knew it. However, I earned $1,000 from Ken Sprague for posing in the Gold Classic, and I intended to use that to get started. Whatever happened, I was determined not to return to the East. I was not yet certain just how I was going to pull it off, but I knew I would stay and make my way somehow.

One afternoon while I was on the beach I was robbed, half the money I had left taken from my pants pocket. A week later, too broke to pay another day's rent, I was forced to move out of my hotel. I started sleeping anywhere I could—in borrowed beds, on park benches, on the beach. There was no problem about being grubby, because I could always clean up and shower at Gold's, where I trained. But being a beach bum was not my style.

I contacted Joe Weider at *Muscle Builder Magaine,* told him I wanted to stay in California and train, and asked if his offer was still open. Joe was delighted. He drew up a contract, rented a car for me, and started paying me a small weekly salary in exchange for my contributions to his magazine and for the right to use my name in his business.

I had to tighten my belt. The money Joe paid me was less than half what I had earned as a sheet-metal worker. Rents in California were high, my grocery bill amounted to much more than the average-sized family spent on food, and most of my clothes had to be custom-made.

One thing my father and I had failed to understand when Joe had offered me contracts before was the principle behind Joe's support of bodybuilders. His philosophy seems to be to give bodybuilders with potential and promise enough financial help for them to be able to train but not so much that they become comfortable with it. It is possible in the bodybuilding game for a few people with talent to make a great living, but you need to be hungry to do it. Joe knows that. My father's first reaction was to assume that Joe was just using me. I did not understand his motives at first either, but it was probably because of them, because of Joe, that I even considered trying out for the part of the Incredible Hulk.

The life of the professional bodybuilder, which I was finally able to live, was perfect for me. It was what I had always wanted, my dream come true. I found myself doing all the things a fifteen-year-old wants to do—only without Mom and Dad shaking a finger and saying don't do this, don't do that.

Living on the edge financially, I continued to have one big fear: that everything would fall through and I would find myself back on the beach, faced with having to return to the East and take up another sheet-metal job, burying myself in my old life forever. That spelled out failure and downfall and meant resuming my old routine.

Among ''The World's Strongest Men''

Meanwhile, I was taking advantage of everything California could offer. I met a girl out in the valley at a club called Big Daddy's. We fell in love and had a pretty solid and satisfying relationship for most of that winter.

Crazy things kept happening to me. Along with a few other guys from the gym I entered the World's Strongest Man Contest. Mostly I did it for fun. I had never trained for sheer strength, but I won fourth place overall and set a world's record in the deadlift— 2,600 pounds. I lifted a car.

It was not the last time I would pick up a car. Sometime later a friend and I went down to Manhattan Beach to catch some sun before a photography session I was scheduled to do. It was a hot day and we were anxious to get to the ocean as soon as possible. About a block from the beach I saw a small space by a fire hydrant, and by nudging my bumper against the car in front of me I was able to park my VW with only about a foot of the rear bumper in the red zone. I decided to take a chance with the police.

A couple of hours later, my friend and I came back to discover that another VW had pulled in behind mine. It was so close I couldn't begin to get out. I was furious. My appointment was with Joe Weider to shoot pictures for the magazine, and I didn't want to be late. There was only one solution. I took hold of the other VW and started to lift it. People stopped on the sidewalk to watch. They could not believe I moved the car up on the curb, setting it almost on top of the fire hydrant.

Just as I finished the owner came running along the street, screaming, "What the hell are you doing to my car?"

At the same moment, a cop drove around the corner. The guy ran out to the police car and started screaming at the cop. The cop told him to shut up.

"Look, officer," I said. "I was just trying to get out of here."

67

"Arrest him," the other guy insisted. "Arrest him. He picked up my car and put it there."

"Nobody can pick up a car," the cop said.

"He did!"

"Look, if you don't shut up I'm going to give you a citation for disturbing the peace. Which will bring it up to four." The cop ticked them off on his fingers. "The first is for parking on the sidewalk. The second is for parking too close to a fire hydrant. The third is for harassing a police officer. Now, do you want to go for five?"

I asked politely if he was through with me.

"Yeah, you're okay, go on."

Training in California was more wonderful than I had ever imagined. Aside from the freedom to work out all day, to have a really effective split routine and enough rest to make it work, there was the warmth and the sunshine. I didn't need to wear heavy sweat clothes all the time to stay warm, and there were not the unbearable hot summers we had had in the East. I could be in shorts and a tank top most of the day. I loved the looks I got from people on the street. They were so taken aback by how big I was they would move aside and let me pass. Just walking to the gym and getting those reactions made me train harder than ever.

I worked all winter getting myself ready for the Olympia. Joe Weider showed up from time to time and gave me advice. I could tell Joe was genuinely impressed, but in one respect he was a lot like my father: He would always pick up on my weak points and encourage me to do more. Joe, too, wanted me to be perfect.

In order to supplement my income and increase my exposure in the bodybuilding world I fit a number of exhibitions into my schedule. Of them all, the most fun was a trip I took to Guadalajara, Mexico, to participate in a show promoted by Roy Velasquez which featured a long list of top-name bodybuilders—including Arnold, Ed Corney, Franco, and Boyer Coe.

I flew to Mexico with Eddie Juliani, Dave Dupre, and Bill Grant. We arrived in the evening, and Velasquez drove us to our hotel. The next morning I woke up starving and went down to the hotel dining room to order breakfast. The waiter could not believe I wanted fourteen eggs, bacon, toast, and coffee. When the food came on a huge platter, it was like a meal for a small platoon of soldiers. The restaurant employees just stood there in amazement and watched me shovel in all that food.

Eddie started getting anxious about going home almost as soon as we arrived. He didn't want to stay any longer than we had to, and he suffered through the days. The morning we were to leave, Eddie looked happier than he had all trip. We went down to load the luggage into the car and start for the airport only to discover that we could not get the car out of the hotel parking garage. There was a parade in the street blocking the exit. A cloud passed

This could get to be a habit

68

over Eddie's face and he became more nervous than ever. He thought it was some kind of conspiracy to keep us there.

"We'll miss our plane," he shouted.

"Great!" I said, to tease him. "We can stay a couple of days and have some more fun."

I went out into the street to watch the parade. Kids noticed me and began asking for my autograph. When someone said they wanted to see my muscles, I pulled off my shirt and started to flex. A couple of other bodybuilders did the same, and a huge crowd circled around to watch us perform. We brought the whole parade to a halt in front of the hotel. This threw Eddie into a panic. He kept trying to get us to stop.

It all worked out, of course. Roy Velasquez pulled a few strings, had another car sent to the hotel, and our plane did not leave without us.

The part of the Incredible Hulk came to me almost out of left field. I was already into the final months of heavy training for the Olympia contest when Universal Studios began casting for the pilot. They contacted gym owners all across the country in an attempt to locate the world's largest bodybuilder. The part didn't sound as though it would take a lot of time, so I went in for an audition. The casting people said they liked me and would be in touch. After two weeks went by and I didn't hear anything I wrote it off.

Actually, that was almost the end of it. Universal had given the part to another person and they were a few days into shooting when something happened to make them reconsider. A little boy, the son of one of the executives, walked on the set and said: "Daddy, that's not the Hulk." That was a serious moment. The Hulk had to be believable, especially to kids, or the show wouldn't work.

That same day Universal called and asked if I could come down for a screen test. I drove to the lot, and the makeup people had me strip down. They worked quickly, gluing on the rubber appliances that would distort my nose and forehead, applying green makeup, and fitting me with a wig of green yak hair. I walked onto the stage where Bill Bixby and the other members of the crew were. Everything stopped. The place grew stone silent. Nobody laughed. Nobody said anything. They were all stunned by my appearance. I removed my robe and started flexing and growling. I saw the producer's face light up. That was it. The next day I was working full-time.

My first full day on the set was a new experience for me—different from bodybuilding or anything else I had ever done, including the filming of *Pumping Iron*. It was my first chance to act, which was something I had wanted to do all my life. It was a nonspeaking part, but a significant part, and I was excited to see what I could do with the character.

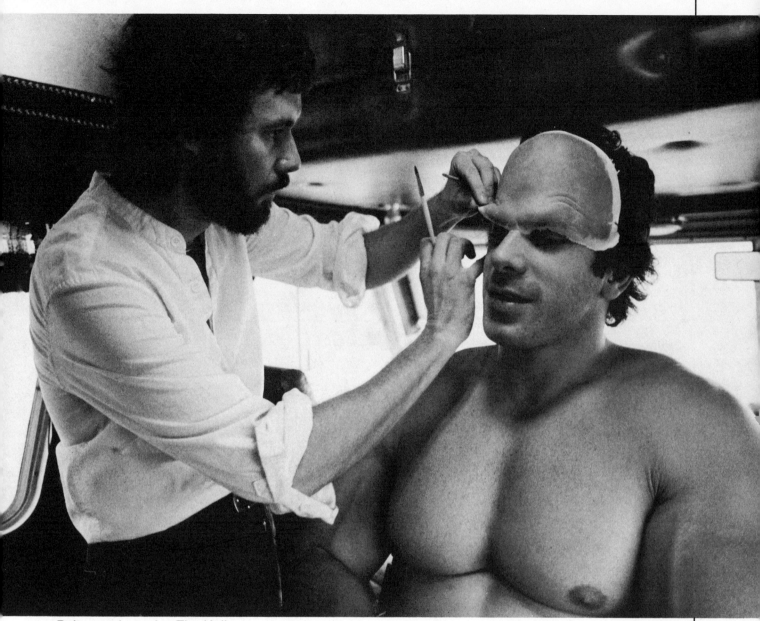

Being made up for *The Hulk*

Bill Bixby had impressed upon me the importance of panto-mime in creating the role and conveying the emotion necessary to give the Hulk the stature we wanted. Pantomime came easy to me, because I had spent a lifetime reading lips and responding to changes in people's expressions in order to know what their feelings were. I had only to reverse the situation to make the Hulk really work. In addition, what I had learned from bodybuilding be-came a great help to me. The years of working in front of mirrors, perfecting this or that move of an exercise, creating and changing my posing routine, made acting that much easier for me. I am convinced that taking those unique and diverse kinds of experi-ences to the part of the Hulk helped win for this character the pop-ularity it now has throughout the world.

Waiting to film *The Hulk*

Walking into the makeup department that first morning and seeing all the different heads on display I found myself thinking about the famous monsters in movie history and the stars who had played them: Lon Chaney, Bela Lugosi, Boris Karloff, Michael Landon, and so on. Stars who had done monster roles had almost all become famous actors. That thought made my work with the Hulk much more challenging, because I wanted to become a famous actor, and disprove a lot of people's speculation that I would never be able to play ordinary roles.

The makeup for the screen test had been hurried and mainly for effect. It was different when I was going on camera; it had to be perfect. Mirrors were adjusted so I could see the makeup being applied. I was mesmerized by the process. I watched myself being changed, becoming a totally different person.

When I stepped out of the motor home into the street I could not believe the reactions I got. I was accustomed to people's stopping and staring at me, but this was different. People were actually intimidated by this green creature. They took a step backward and their mouths dropped open.

I kept touching myself: Was I dreaming? Was I really doing this? Each time I passed a mirror on the set I would go into shock. This green guy with a huge nose and a lumpy forehead stared back at me. I felt like a caveman.

At some point during the first few days of filming I realized I had a serious decision to make. I could either be the Hulk or I could continue to train and compete in the Mr. Olympia contest, but I couldn't do both. I had assumed at first that I could bring some weights onto the set and get in some workout time between shots. That was impossible, because I always had to be in green makeup and I had to avoid touching myself or moving too much to keep from smearing it. Then, too, the days, which I had assumed would not exceed eight hours, were rarely *only* eight hours. They usually stretched into twelve-hour, fourteen-hour, even sixteen-hour days.

At the gym everyone said I had made a big mistake. "Green?" they said. "You've got to be painted green?" They thought I was crazy. "What kind of part is that, Lou? You don't say anything—you just growl and throw people around."

But to me it was much more. I knew I could do a lot with the character. Although I had no lines to say, I was going to make the Hulk speak. It was a chance to use my body, to show it to the best advantage. It was also an opportunity to become a hero and be identified with heroic deeds. That had been one of my biggest dreams.

I let the guys at the gym say what they wanted. None of it bothered me. My big concern was breaking the news to Joe Weider. I had spent years working toward the goal of winning the Mr. Olympia title; it was the pinnacle in bodybuilding, the finest achievement in the sport, and I knew I could win it. It was the first time I had spent an entire year on training and refinement. Joe, too, believed I could win. He had invested in me, and my win would be a boost for the work we did together in the magazine.

After about three weeks of working long hours and only being able to slip into the gym for a short time each evening, I walked into Joe's office and said, "Joe, you're going to be really pissed at me, but I can't keep training for the competition."

I thought I was going to have to fight with him, but Joe was very understanding—as he has always been in all of our dealings. He just said he hoped I had made the right decision and advised me to stay active in bodybuilding because he wanted to continue our association.

Of course, Joe knew I would never quit bodybuilding. It is as much a part of me as breathing and eating, and always will be. But the Hulk made it necessary for me to retire from active competition. It was a difficult decision to make, but I saw that in the long run I would benefit more from using my bodybuilding and skills as a bodybuilder in acting.

Just before I began work on *The Incredible Hulk* I met and married my first wife. It was one of those strange situations that happen out of a change of mood and circumstance. Sue was dating a friend of mine. All spring they had been having problems, which I had heard exclusively from my friend's side. Then one night at the gym, she told me her story. I was sympathetic, but I couldn't tell her what to do. She said she understood that and she thanked me for listening. A short time later my friend left to go back to the East Coast. Sue stayed. She called me one day and asked if I would have a cup of coffee with her. We became good friends and started dating. Then we were married. We were together during the first difficult months of my work on *The Incredible Hulk*. I was working too hard and away from home too much. I think those long hours would have been difficult on any marriage. Ours lasted 364 days.

The Incredible Hulk had taken over my life. I don't say that disparagingly—because I allowed it to do so. I saw it as a unique opportunity, and I applied myself to making everything I could of the character. I was continually trying to work out ways to improve him, asking myself what he would think, how he would act in different situations. I wanted to make the Hulk more than a green creature, to keep him fresh and challenging.

I am never satisfied with what I do in anything. I strive for perfection, knowing it is impossible and therefore the biggest challenge. I think this drive came to me as a result of my years in bodybuilding, and I brought it to acting. I regularly watched the completed *Incredible Hulk* shows and analyzed them, trying to be objective and learn all I could. I have discovered the camera angles that are best for me, the shots that really work. I didn't mind telling the director when I felt a shot wasn't going to have much impact or how I would change it to make it better.

My greatest concern in filming *The Incredible Hulk* was the stuntwork—both for my own safety and the success of the show. I think the stunts involving the Hulk are, along with the David Banner story, the reason the series has continued to be so popular. They are heroic actions, the kind of superhuman deeds I dreamed of doing as a child.

I perform most of my own stunts. I have broken through walls, run through windows, and smashed different things. I love scenes in which I throw people around; I like to fantasize that it is someone I dislike.

One of the first stuntmen I worked with came to do a scene in which I had to throw him into the water. The shot of him going into the water was done from a trampoline. Then we started shooting the part where I picked him up to throw him. We were on a scaffold about twelve feet high. I had hold of the back of his pants, ready to heave him, and I checked the placement of the big airbag on which he was going to land. I said, "I've got a feeling you'll go farther than that."

"I know you bodybuilders," he said. "You aren't as strong as you look."

"You'd better listen to me. I'm really strong at heaving."

"I've been in this business twenty-five years," he argued. "Take my word for it, I know what I'm talking about."

"Come on!" the director yelled. "We're rolling."

I heaved the guy as hard as I could, which is what the script called for. He sailed fifteen feet beyond the airbag and hit the concrete. He picked himself up, looked at me, and said, "This is the last time I work with that man." Then he limped away.

Later, there was a scene in which I had to fight a bear in water. The bear was named Pooh. He was still a baby, but he was seven feet tall and weighed four hundred pounds. My first scene was to wrestle him underwater. The director gave the signal from the bank, and I went underwater, rolling around with the bear. Then I came up out of the water and gave a growl. Everyone in the crew burst out laughing. I wondered what was the matter. Then I saw someone pointing at my head. I reached up and discovered that the bear had pulled off my wig, leaving me as bald as Kojak. I was furious. I turned around and socked this huge bear. He looked at me and ran back to the bank. It was the last shot we could do that day, because the bear refused to come back into the water with me.

I did not see any of my actual work as the Hulk until the initial screening of the pilot, months after we began shooting. I invited Joe and Betty Weider to attend as my guests. Walking into Projector Room One at Universal Studios, where there were about a hundred people, I was suddenly overcome by mixed emotions: I wanted to see the picture and I didn't want to see it. Although I knew it would be good I was afraid it might not be.

The first time I saw the Hulk loom up on the screen I was stunned, and after each closeup of the face, I sat frozen in my seat. The creature was me and it was not me. I had transformed it into something awesome, something almost too real.

The show ended. I just sat there, still unable to move. I didn't know what to think. Joe was sitting beside me, applauding away. His favorite pose in bodybuilding display is the Most Muscular Pose. Each time I came onto the screen, crouched into that pose, and growled, he would start jumping up and down in his seat. Even before the lights had come up Joe cried out that it was fantastic, it was going to be a smash. He was really excited. He said it would do more for bodybuilding than anything in the history of the sport; the next day he was telling everyone that *The Incredible Hulk* was destined to be a hit.

Joe was right. *The Incredible Hulk* did become a hit. When it went on the air the national ratings skyrocketed. I knew then that I had made the right decision—again. And it had changed my life.

One thing that did not improve with that success was my marriage. After it fell apart, I was forced to do some serious thinking about the direction my life had taken. There were no problems with my career. I was beginning to see that I had a future in show business, that I would have to work at it but it was there. On the other hand, my private life was a shambles. I did not know how to have a successful relationship with a woman. In fact, I had barely learned how to make friends with women, let alone having any idea how to go about treating a woman as an equal. My biggest downfall, which was due to a lack of experience and probably a certain bitterness I held because of countless rejections by girls when I was a young man, was my macho approach. I was strong and physical and failed to understand that a good reciprocal relationship could not work under those conditions.

The person who really set me straight on this was Carla Green. One night I took some friends to a club called TGI Friday's and said I wanted a table. They asked if I had a reservation, and when I said no, they said they were full. I was insulted. I had been there a number of times and I had never had any trouble getting in—there or anyplace. After they insisted there was no table, I asked to speak with the manager. The manager was Carla Green, a striking blonde who came out of the back and said very matter-of-factly: "I'm sorry, Mr. Ferrigno, there are no tables. We can't seat you." I argued with her, but she would not give an inch. I stormed out of the club and took my friends someplace else.

I had promised myself I would never go back to TGI Friday's, but for some reason I kept thinking about Carla Green; she was sharp-looking and I had been attracted to her. Once I cooled down I realized she had just been doing her job. Finally, a few weeks later, I went in with Manuel Perry, my stunt double from the series. There was no trouble with tables that time. I saw Carla. She seemed even more attractive than I had remembered, and I asked her to come to the table and sit down with us. She was more re-

Carla and me

laxed than before. We got into a conversation. I kept looking hard at her in order to read her lips, and she confessed later that something about this struck her.

I asked her out, and we began seeing each other regularly. Carla was different from any girl I had ever dated. Each time I came on with my old macho act she would stand up to me and tell me to cool it. She said nothing about me frightened her. The first time she talked this way to me I was infuriated. I didn't say anything, but inside I was fuming. Luckily, I realized how right she was, and that made me want to see her more than ever. Carla didn't mind telling me when I was wrong; but she was also warm and understanding. She was a special person who treated me as I had never been treated before.

In the same way *The Incredible Hulk* had changed my professional life, Carla Green totally changed my private life. The next spring we were married, and Carla started helping me in everything I did. Because of her experience in business she became my manager and began to untangle the loose ends of my entire career, including my extensive mail-order business and the personal-instruction programs I periodically put together for people who want special attention.

There was one sad note, however. After we were married a doctor explained to Carla that it would be very difficult for us to have children. We wanted children, and that came as a blow to us. We began doing everything we could to correct the problem. The doctor continued to maintain that the chances of a child were slim. Then in the fall of 1980 he told her she was pregnant.

When I came home from the studio that night she broke the news to me. I went white as a sheet.

"Are you all right, Louie?"

"Yes." But I was suddenly frightened. I was happy and frightened at the same time. Looking back on it, the whole thing seems comical. I had broken through walls, wrestled with a bear, lifted a car. I was one of the biggest bodybuilders in the world and one of the strongest men in the world, but I couldn't handle this situation. Carla told me to sit down, and she began to comfort me, to tell me that everything would be all right, not to worry. I couldn't believe it. I was going to be a father. Our daughter, Shanna Victoria, was born on June 13, 1981.

For me *The Incredible Hulk* will always stand as a milestone in my career. I can look back on it as the part that brought everything together, my childhood dreams, my years of work as a bodybuilder, and my ambition to be an actor. It provided me with the world's greatest acting class. I had to learn to be comfortable in front of a camera while the ink was still drying on my contract. In the hundreds of episodes I had the opportunity to observe firsthand the work of a number of great actors and actresses. Watching them step into the lights and pick up a scene was like magic. I analyzed what they did as carefully as I would have gleaned any-

thing from a stack of textbooks and lecture notes. From their example, I tried to do more than the script called for, learning to laugh and cry, to shed real tears, without being able to speak a word. In the process the Hulk and his mission have become close to me.

When it came time for me to perform my first speaking part in *The Incredible Hulk*—I played both the Hulk and the part of another character in an episode called "King of the Beach"—I was ready.

At first, the idea of all those lines made me nervous. However, from the moment the director called for action I felt something inside me begin to take over. And when I got into my customary makeup and played the scenes of the Hulk I felt I was a different person. I got to the point after three days of shooting where I was memorizing eight to ten pages of dialogue each morning and then going through the whole day of shooting without missing a word. That accomplishment made me feel certain that the career I saw for myelf in show business was much more than my own fantasy. I knew I could move on into other roles. I had felt something I would not forget. I knew then that I was an actor. I had passed another milestone, one that almost everyone who had known me as a child would have said I could not have achieved. But I had learned to believe that no handicap could keep me from what I really wanted. I had opened another door and seen that there were endless rooms before me.

I believe we each have a destiny. Within certain people is a desire to rise up, no matter what the opposition, and find their way to the top. We must only discover our methods and tools. For me, those were bodybuilding. Training brought out in me everything that was good: desire and ambition, as well as a sense of the strong person I could become. It provided a constant challenge and educated me about goal setting and positive thinking. In the gym I learned to love hard work and its rewards both physically and mentally. I taught myself to be a winner and to realize that, above all else, strength is my business.

PICTURE PORTFOLIO

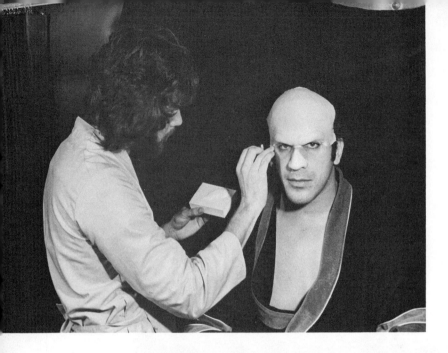

PART
TWO

1

BODYBUILDING—A FOUNDATION FOR THE FUTURE

Bodybuilding is an ancient discipline which was once practiced by great men in almost every walk of life, including philosophers and important figures in government. In those ancient cultures it was considered a mark of excellence to be fit in mind, body, and spirit. These people knew that the correspondence and balance between these elements not only made a person function on a higher level of efficiency but acted as a kind of insurance against all forms of illness and even despondency.

Gradually, in the Western world the emphasis on physical development was minimized—except among athletes and men whose employment was labor or war. Fortunately, in the last decade, through the efforts of many of my colleagues and friends, such as Arnold Schwarzenegger, Joe Weider, Bill Pearl, and a handful of other dedicated professional bodybuilders, bodybuilding has been elevated to a new level of respectability among men and women.

Today, gyms across the country are filled with men and women from all walks of life. I believe this is a significant omen. A country is only as strong as its people. I feel that by striking a balance between the physical, the mental, and the spiritual we can be prepared for anything.

When I first began bodybuilding, I was laughed at and called names, but I knew what I wanted and let that desire for success carry me beyond criticism and on to win the Mr. America, Mr. International, and Mr. Universe titles. The goals I made fifteen years ago as a teenage bodybuilder are still at the heart of everything I do today—from my work as an actor to my interests in instructing and producing.

Successful bodybuilding is not easy. It gives back only in proportion to the hard work that you put into it. To get the best results, you must be dedicated and motivated. But the hours you spend working out can and will pay handsome dividends.

You can make bodybuilding anything you wish. It can be your sport, your workout, your aerobic routine. Aside from being the best all-around discipline for total body fitness and conditioning, it

99

can serve to strengthen selected areas of the body for participants in other sports. It can condition the legs for skiers and runners, the arms and legs for tennis, baseball, handball, and squash—in fact, most of today's top professional athletes engage in some kind of weight training.

I will only make one promise about my program: You will get from my kind of bodybuilding exactly what you are willing to take from it. This may be specialized training for a particular purpose: increased strength, coordination, and conditioning. It may be therapeutic (to overcome the debilitating effects of injury or illness). Or it may be your profession, if that is what you choose. If you have the ambition and the drive you can achieve anything you wish. But those are the promises and commitments you must make to yourself.

The dividends I mentioned earlier are those additional benefits you did not have in mind when you began working out with weights. Aside from increased muscle size, strength, and endurance, your overall appearance will improve along with your sense of self-confidence. Self-confidence comes from personal success. Your progress in bodybuilding can be easily measured in gains and losses, pounds and repetitions. The success that comes from this initial progress can be immeasurable. In this respect, I hope the example of what I have been able to accomplish in my own life will be a source of inspiration to you.

MENTAL ATTITUDE

The beginning of any program is in the mind. Your mental attitude, as well as a realistic plan of action, is the indicator of how successful you will be. In bodybuilding a positive mental attitude is especially necessary if you are to reach your goals. You must believe in yourself and your ability to succeed. Once you have done that unshakably, you can only go forward and upward.

The kind of positive mental attitude necessary for bodybuilding is more than a belief in some eventual success. Belief is a beginning, but you must be so committed that you can actually visualize your gains long before they happen. You must see yourself working and growing. In your mind you will have a sharp image of yourself with a smaller waist, a larger chest, more powerful arms; in short, you will see yourself transformed into the person you desire to become. The small goals you achieve over the next two weeks, two months, or two years will merely be steppingstones your mind has placed to help you toward your ultimate goal.

GOALS

We all know what goals are, but we don't all know how or why they work. In bodybuilding you need two kinds of goals: big goals, or milestones, and small goals, or steppingstones. The milestones

are those ultimate goals where you see yourself standing on the dais accepting the Mr. Universe trophy or you see yourself cut down from a sloppy fat 230 pounds to a trim 168. Steppingstones are the small goals such as losing 5 to 7 pounds next week or decreasing your waist measurement an inch in three weeks or gaining ½ inch of arm measurement after only twenty workout days.

Nothing positive, solid, or lasting is gained without definite goals and the driving force to realize them. Goals are not goals unless they are taken seriously. In bodybuilding there are three devices to help achieve your goals and stay on a success schedule:

1. Training diary.
2. Photographs.
3. Daily reminders.

TRAPEZIUS

DELTOID

PECTORALS

BICEPS

ABDOMINALS

FOREARM

WRIST

QUADRICEPS

REAR DELTOID

LATS

UPPER BACK

LOWER BACK

TRICEPS

LEG BICEPS

CALVES

Training Diary

Any notebook will serve as a training diary. Its purpose is to provide a written record of your workouts. List the time you went into the gym, the exercises you did, the numbers of sets and repetitions, plus the number of pounds of iron you used, and the time you left the gym. If you are working on a crash weight-loss or weight-gain program, you should also record the food you eat each day and the number of calories you consume.

Photographs

A camera is an invaluable investment for a bodybuilder—or at least the film for a friend's camera. I suggest you shoot photographs of yourself when you begin and then at ten-day or two-week intervals thereafter. Always use the same lens and approximately the same angle; if you can, stand in the same spot for all the photographs. You can often fool yourself in a mirror, but a straightforward photograph hides very little.

Daily Reminders

Reminders are written statements of your goals. They should be written on cards and placed where you can see them at various times during the day. For instance, goals to do with weight loss or weight gain can be effective if you place them on your refrigerator

door. Other reminders can be taped to mirrors, the dashboard of your car, on your desk at work, or any other place where you will see them. Positive reminders always work best for me. I avoid using the word *don't* in them. They can be simple statements: "A 33-inch waist!" "190 pounds on May 1!" "Mr. America, 1985!" "Legs!"

As you advance you will find that your goals change. For instance, in the case of muscle size you increase most rapidly in the beginning. Later, as you begin to reach your potential, your inch-size gains slow down. Once you have gained most of your muscle mass, your goals should be directed toward muscle quality, or more strength and power. However, with the confidence you have gained by that time, you will probably no longer need to be reinforced by such obvious visual progress.

NUTRITION

In any kind of building, the final result reflects the basic materials you put in. These can make the difference between a mansion and a shack, a luxury automobile and the economy model. It is no different in bodybuilding. I believe that nutrition is 70 percent of bodybuilding success. Food is used by the body for all growth. In building muscle it is important to choose the kinds of foods that will work with exercise to give the best results.

We all need a balance of proteins, carbohydrates, and fats. For the bodybuilder (and this goes for most people as well) the best balance is a diet high in good-quality proteins, high in good-quality carbohydrates, and relatively low in fats. Protein foods such as fish, chicken, meat, eggs, and dairy products are essential in growth and repair of muscle tissue; the carbohydrates in fresh vegetables, fresh fruit, and whole-grain products provide us with energy. Fat is necessary for proper body function. However, few diets contain too little fat. Fats come in two types—saturated and unsaturated. For the best health you should restrict your intake as much as possible to unsaturated fats, which are found in fish, fish products, and vegetable oils such as safflower, soybean, corn, and sunflower oil.

VITAMINS

The body depends upon obtaining all of its nutrients from various food sources. However, your daily food consumption may not provide your body with all of these essential nutrients, especially if you are training to build muscle. Therefore, many people try to fortify their diets with vitamin and mineral supplements. I use supplements and recommend their use if it is done prudently and with every effort to maintain a proper chemical balance in the body. The problem with this is that many people overdo it, taking vitamins and minerals in huge quantities which can be harmful.

Unlike fats and proteins, vitamins carry out their nutritional role in very small concentrations. However, they do *not* work alone in our bodies; they are part of the overall enzyme system. They should always be taken with a meal.

Vitamin A assists in growth and repair of body tissue, keeps the skin supple and smooth, protects the membrane linings of the mouth, nose, and lungs, and reduces the incidence of infection. I ordinarily take 10,000 USP units of A and increase this during contest training.

Vitamin D functions with calcium and phosphorus in maintaining a strong skeletal system. It is essential to the proper functioning of the thyroid gland and is also a factor in blood clotting. Most foods do not contain an appreciable amount of Vitamin D, but sunshine, working on the natural oils of the skin, will stimulate the body to produce its own Vitamin D. I supplement this with 400 USP units of Vitamin D.

Vitamin E. The essential function of Vitamin E is the regulation of the metabolism of the cell nuclei. Its main functions are to assist in healing and to protect the red blood cells and vital hormones from oxygenation. I take 200 IU per day.

Vitamin B Complex. The B vitamins are: B_1 (thiamine), B_2 (riboflavin), B_6 (pyridoxine), B_{12} (cyanocobalamin), B_{15} (pangamic acid), biotin, choline, folic acid, inositol, niacin and pantothenic acid. They function together to convert carbohydrates into glucose, which the body uses to produce energy; they are important to the skin and hair, and the need for them increases during infection, sickness, or stress. I take a multicap which provides me with 10 mg each of B_1, B_2, B_6, 25 mcg of B_{12}, 100 mg of niacin, 1 mg of folic acid, 130 mg of pantothenic acid, 100 mg of choline, 30 mcg of inositol, plus B_{15} and PABA.

Vitamin C helps to build and maintain the skeletal system and aids in the production of connective tissue. The need for Vitamin C increases when the body is under any kind of stress: infection, fatigue, injury, surgery or burns. This is why massive short-term doses are often prescribed when recovering from an illness. I take 500 to 1000 mg a day.

MINERALS

I take my minerals in multicap form, which provides a balance of the following nutrients.

Calcium builds strong bones and teeth. It works with Vitamins D and K in blood clotting and with the B vitamins to fight stress and nervous disorders.

Magnesium combines with calcium and phosphorus to strengthen bones and teeth, maintain the nervous system and assist in muscle functions.

Zinc is important to circulation, healing, and healthy skin.

Iron helps the body utilize oxygen and prevent anemia.

Copper is important to circulation and healthy blood.

Manganese serves as a catalyst for the metabolic processes.

Potassium functions to regulate the fluids in the body and help bring nutrients into the blood.

REST

In order to grow and develop at an accelerated rate, your body needs plenty of rest. In addition to vigorous exercise and a sound diet, you should try to get eight to ten hours of sleep a day. Relaxation is not only necessary to your general well-being, it also gives your muscle tissues time to repair and grow.

You can adjust your schedule so your workout times help promote a more relaxed way of life. For some of you this will mean training in the morning so you can approach the day more calmly. Others will want to train in the evening to release those tensions that have built up during the day.

Although I strongly advocate training in the gym only every other day (the reasons for this are thoroughly explained in a later section), I suggest you do some kind of stretching every day. Stretching allows your muscles to relax and grow.

INSTINCTIVE TRAINING

The great bodybuilders have always relied on what we call the principle of instinctive training. Nobody responds exactly the same way to every exercise, diet, or training schedule. To find your best personal routine, you must consider the information from your training diary, including the record of your measurements and your periodic photographs.

One important aspect of instinctive training is biofeedback, which is the pertinent information your body tells you about itself. Listen to these signals. Their function in bodybuilding is to pass on information about how your body is responding to exercise.

An obvious positive signal of a good workout is a muscle pump. This is a full, tight sensation in the muscle which happens as a result of the blood rushing to an area that has just been worked. Once you've had a pump you will realize why your favorite bodybuilders talk about the pump the way they do. It is almost as if you can feel actual growth.

Another sign of a good workout is morning-after muscle soreness. This tells you that the muscle tissue has been broken down and is being repaired. This is the natural process for normal muscle growth. However, if the soreness is in your joints, tendons, or ligaments, it is likely you have been overdoing it, using too much weight or performing an exercise incorrectly.

Instinctive training does not happen overnight. It takes time to cultivate your instincts and key them with your reactions. You can begin with something as simple as monitoring soreness and calculating your progress from the results of your diary and the photographs you have taken at spaced intervals. As your confidence grows and you learn more about your body, you will instinctively begin to know how to improve your training techniques. This is the mark of a progressive bodybuilder.

DRUGS

No book on modern bodybuilding techniques is complete without a discussion of drugs. Personally, I am opposed to any kind of drugs, especially those used to obtain accelerated results in bodybuilding. The drugs used in bodybuilding are called anabolic steroids. Some bodybuilders do take them. Although it is true that they can help to increase body weight, they have serious disadvantages that in my opinion make them undesirable.

Anabolic steroids are artificial counterparts of testosterone, the male sex hormone. One of the prime functions of testosterone is to increase and accelerate muscle growth, a process called anabolism. Herein lies the basic reason why men are able to gain incredible muscularity and women cannot.

In your body there is a natural regulatory function called the negative feedback mechanism. One of the things it does is to regulate the production of testosterone. Your body cannot distinguish between the natural testosterone and the anabolic steroids. When you introduce steroids into your system the regulatory center automatically cuts back on natural testosterone production. Therefore in order to maintain an accelerated growth rate you must add more steroids.

There are a number of problems with creating this imbalance in your system. When you stop taking steroids it will take your body a number of weeks to resume normal hormone production. One of the effects of this is a rapid degeneration of muscle tissue. Many bodybuilders see this happening and immediately get back on steroids. In effect, they become addicted. Although research is still being done, there is evidence that some side effects of taking steroids are hypertension, liver degeneration, hair loss, and impotence—all serious hazards to good health. For these reasons I advocate drug-free bodybuilding. Drug dependence is a weakness; bodybuilding is something you do to become strong. In my mind, there is no logical way the two work together.

CLOTHING

Be comfortable. That is probably the most important thing to be said about training clothes. Most of the time you will only want to wear trunks and a T-shirt or tank top. Sweat suits are fine—especially in cold weather. I personally like to see the results of my workout, and therefore I train in only shorts and tank top. One note worth mentioning: If you have faults—if your waist is fat or you have skinny legs—don't simply cover them up with a sweat suit. Be honest with yourself. Expose your faults so you know exactly what you are working to overcome.

REPS AND SETS

Two terms you need to know to understand the exercises are *rep* and *set*. A rep—that is, a repetition—is one full movement of an exercise. If you do 10 Push-ups, you have performed 10 reps of the Push-up.

A set is a series of reps of a simple exercise with no interruption or break between them.

Typically the exercise numbers will be written like this: "2 sets of 8 reps." This means you would do a total of 16 repetitions with one short break between them.

DEDICATION AND DRIVE

To succeed in bodybuilding you must have determination and dedication. I know from years of experience that this is a difficult and demanding sport. There are days when it is easy to find excuses not to go to the gym or reasons to do fewer repetitions of an exercise or even to drop an entire set. This is dangerous negative thinking you should avoid. When you catch yourself backsliding, reverse the situation by telling yourself how great it will feel to take hold of the barbell, how anxious you are to add 10 more pounds or another rep.

BODYBUILDING AS A UNIQUE LIFE-STYLE

Whether or not you intend to become a professional in the sport, I predict that bodybuilding will profoundly change your life. I have seen this happen with hundreds of people. After a few weeks or months in the gym you will find yourself thinking differently about yourself. Your ideas about eating will change. You will have a different outlook on the people with whom you associate. Bodybuilding has such a positive effect that it seems to drive people on toward their goals and becomes a source of inspiration.

RULES AND REMINDERS

1. Perform the exercises as they are given. Follow the directions and do not skip steps or try to take shortcuts. There are no shortcuts in bodybuilding.
2. Make a time commitment for working out and then *do not miss workouts*—except in the case of illness.
3. Do not be too eager to move from the basic bodybuilding program to the intermediate one. Like any building, bodybuilding requires time and patience.
4. Set short-range and long-range goals. Use them to gauge your progress.
5. Be positive. Look at every pound of weight you add to the bar and every additional rep you do as a significant step forward. Think only of success.
6. Associate with people in the gym who will inspire you to do more, work harder, and become better.
7. Be strong in everything you undertake in the gym and out of the gym.
8. Take pride in your efforts as a bodybuilder. Be a credit to the sport.

2

COMPLETE PRE-GYM CONDITIONING PROGRAM FOR BEGINNERS AND YOUNG BODYBUILDERS

BEGINNING BODYBUILDERS

This program fulfills two purposes. It is ideal as a conditioning program for anyone who has never worked out, and it is an essential and adequate program for any aspiring young bodybuilder under the age of thirteen.

I do not believe anyone younger than thirteen should train with heavy weights. This is not to say you should forget about training. But you should use only the weight of your own body—which is perfectly adequate. After all, if you weigh 85 pounds, a Push-up is approximately the equivalent of doing a bench press with an 85-pound barbell.

The reasons I do not advocate heavy weights for young bodybuilders have to do mostly with their future. If you are young, you are still growing. Your joints and tendons are developing, assuming form and position, and heavy training might cause injuries or misalignment. However, the freehand exercises in the following section, which combine your body weight with stretching, are perfect to enhance proper growth as well as to increase your overall strength, coordination, and agility.

TEENAGE BODYBUILDERS

Chapter 15 is devoted to this age group. Teenagers, like younger bodybuilders, are still growing; they can train with weights but should be extra-careful to do the exercises properly and without too much weight.

ADULT BEGINNERS

If you are an adult and starting bodybuilding, the series of freehand exercises given in this chapter will be a great way to limber up, stretch out, and prepare your muscles for the work you will be doing in gym. Perform these exercises for a minimum of

ten days or until you can do them in a continuous, rhythmical series for at least thirty minutes before you consider starting with weights.

Remember what I said about doing an exercise correctly. To my mind this is the secret of great bodybuilding. Get the form down first; then you can really bomb your muscles with hard work. But even then you should never allow yourself to become sloppy, never handle more weight than you can with full strong movement. That is the time you are most susceptible to injury.

TIME AND PLACE

Choose a time and a place where you can work out without interruption. The success of any training program is greater if you can give it your undivided attention. Concentration and dedication are two valuable assets in bodybuilding, and if you can learn them early you are already assured of succeeding.

Bodybuilding is not easy. It takes a conscious effort on your part. However, there are things you can do to make it easier. Setting a schedule is one. I know from experience that the body responds best to set schedules. Once you tell yourself a particular time—seven in the morning on Monday, Wednesday, and Friday, for example—you have overcome one obstacle to training. You must convince yourself that those times are *only* for working out. Then you encourage yourself by creating a positive attitude toward the workout time. Remind yourself how terrific you felt after your first session. Remember the exhilarating feeling it gave you. Tell yourself you are anxious to add another rep to your Reverse Chins or to do five more Sit-ups.

INSPIRE YOURSELF

Inspire yourself. You will be doing this first series at home. Perhaps you can set aside a place where you can put up a poster or a few photographs of your heroes. We have all had them. One of my early heroes, as you will remember, was Larry Scott; for Arnold Schwarzenegger it was Reg Park, the great South African bodybuilder. Sometimes studying these inspirational photographs makes it easier to visualize your own goals.

Restrict your training to three sessions per week. Do not allow yourself to get into your exercise routine on the "off" days. If you want to do something, try jogging or biking or just taking a long, brisk walk. Then one day a week, preferably on a Sunday or another day when you are not working or going to school, give your body a complete rest.

EQUIPMENT

You will need only a chinning bar and a 2×4 block for this series. There are chinning bars available which are inexpensive and can be temporarily placed between the jambs of any ordinary doorway.

118

FREEHAND EXERCISES

THE WARM-UP

A warm-up period is an essential beginning to every good exercise session. It gets your blood moving and prepares your body for the harder work that is to come.

Begin warming up with some slow, simple body movements to loosen your torso. Stand with your feet spread. Start with a small amount of movement and gradually increase the rotation. At first allow your entire body to move so that you feel it in your ankles, knees, and hips. Then keep your legs and hips from moving and swing only your upper body. The movement should not be fast, and should be smooth and rhythmical. Inhale and exhale deeply and fully as you move. I have included photographs of four floor exercises I use to stretch my muscles and prepare me for my workout.

SHOULDER STAND
From a position with your back flat on the floor, roll up onto your shoulders until your legs are extended straight above you in the air. Rest your weight on your shoulders and support yourself with your hands at the small of your back. Now stretch your toes up as far as you can toward the ceiling without moving your shoulders or arms from their position on the floor. Hold for a few seconds and breathe normally.

LOWER BACK STRETCH
Lying flat on your back, lift your legs up and back until they are extended over your head parallel to the floor. Keeping your arms extended along the floor, stretch the muscles in your lower back and thighs by slowly lowering your toes toward the floor. Hold for a few seconds and breathe normally.

TOE TOUCHES
Keeping your legs extended straight before you, grab your toes and stretch forward as far as you can without straining, ideally until your chest touches your legs. Hold for a moment.

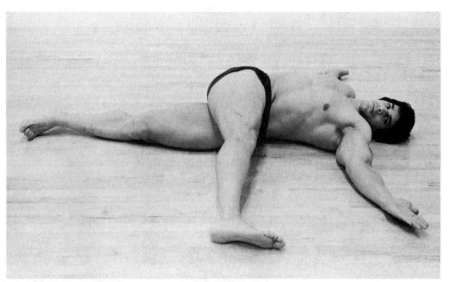

SCISSORS STRETCH
Lying on your back on the floor with your arms extended straight out from the shoulders, cross your right thigh over your left thigh and stretch your leg up as far as you can toward your hand without bending your knee, as in the picture. Hold for a moment and then repeat with the other leg.

Next, moving slowly, reach up as high as you can and come down to touch the floor. If you cannot touch the floor, just go as far as you can. *Do not bounce;* bouncing tightens your muscles and tortures your ligaments and tendons. Stretch the muscles slowly, thoroughly. Return slowly to the full upright position. Repeat at least ten times. It may take two or three reps before you can actually touch the floor, or it may take a week. Don't worry about it. Just go down a little farther each time. And count each inch as progress. Eventually, you should be able to put the palm of your hand flat on the floor without bending your knees. Two or three minutes of stretching should loosen your body sufficiently to allow you to move on to the first exercise.

120

LEGS

I am a fanatic about training legs. The muscles in the legs are the most neglected of any muscle group in the body. Legs are the weak point of many of the great competing bodybuilders. In fact, many contestants have won because of their legs.

The Squat

Probably the most effective all-around exercise for this entire muscle group is the Squat. In addition to its work in the leg area, the Squat is fantastic for toning up your digestive organs, promoting good breathing, and giving a boost to your circulatory system.

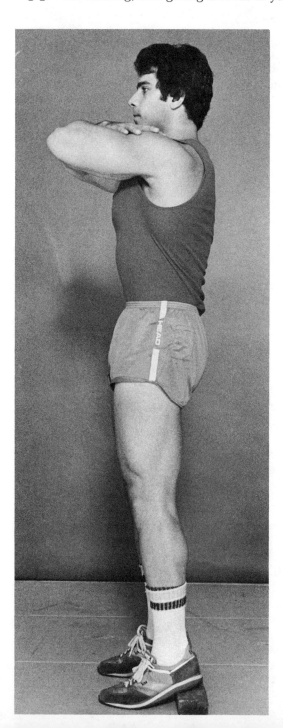

This will be the full squat with only your body weight. Stand with your feet approximately 1 foot apart and with your heels comfortably on a short length of 2×4; this will help keep your back straight and assist you in maintaining your balance. Hold your head up, look straight ahead, and let your body down until your thighs are parallel to the floor. Pause briefly, then push your body up to the starting position. Hold your back straight throughout this exercise. Inhale as you go down, exhale as you come up.

Begin with 2 sets of 8 reps.

The Lunge

Lunges are one of the most effective thigh builders. Work on learning proper form with this simple Lunge using only your body weight. Later in the course you can add the weight of a barbell and really blast your legs.

Begin from the upright position, as you see in the first photograph, then step out smoothly and evenly with your right foot. Allow your left foot to remain on the starting line and your left knee to go down until it barely touches the floor. Maintaining a smooth rhythm, return to the original position and repeat the above movements with your left leg.

Do 1 set of 10 reps with each leg.

The Calf Raise

The Calf Raise is the only exercise that will fully develop the calf muscle. Most bodybuilders concentrate on their upper bodies, but the calves can be the most impressive feature of a well-developed physique. The gastrocnemius and soleus muscles which make up the calf often seem slow to respond. The reason for this is usually the bodybuilder's failure to realize how much work they really need. People walk and climb stairs regularly, so the calf muscles are always being used. In order to make significant changes you should really work this muscle.

You will need a chair and the 2×4 block you used for the Squat. Position yourself a foot or so from the chair with the toes of your right foot up on the 2×4 block. Holding the back of the chair for balance, raise your left foot as you see in the first photograph. Lift yourself as far up on the toes of your right foot as you can. Pause briefly in the extreme position. *Slowly* lower yourself until your heel touches the floor.

Repeat 10 times. Change to left foot. Perform 10 reps; 10 reps with both calves constitutes 1 set. Rest a few seconds and do another set.

NOTE: It is important that all the movements of this exercise be done *slowly* and smoothly, that you keep your back straight, and that you get no assistance from your hands.

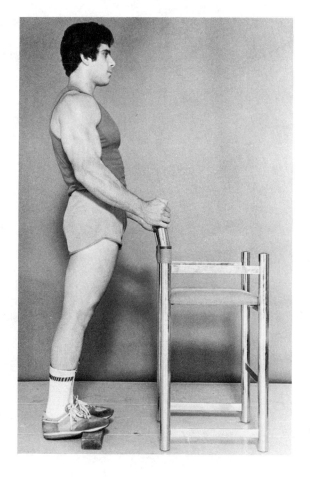
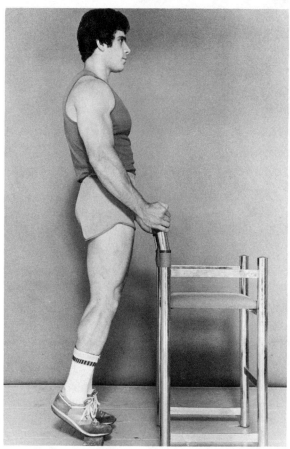

The Push-up

Push-ups work to firm up the muscles in the chest (pectorals) and shoulders (deltoids) and give some toning to the triceps. This is a familiar exercise, but it is often abused. Follow the directions as I give them and you will get the full benefit of the Push-up.

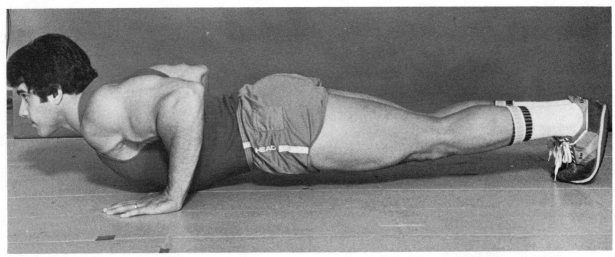

Lie on your stomach on the floor with your hands parallel and at approximately shoulder width. Keep your body straight, and push up until your arms are locked. Hold for the count of two. Let yourself slowly back down until your chest just touches the floor. If you do the movements of this exercise slowly you will feel that letting yourself down becomes as much work as pushing up. This is called negative resistance and is a valuable though often overlooked aspect of bodybuilding. Exhale as you push up; inhale as you let yourself back to the floor.

Start with 1 set of 10 reps, build up to 2 sets of 10 reps.

Chin-ups

Three variations of the Chin-up will effectively work the latissimus dorsi and the trapezius (the major muscles of the back), as well as the deltoids (the shoulders) and to a lesser extent the biceps (the arms). Again, this series of variations can be at least twice as effective if they are executed properly. This means working at a smooth moderate pace with careful attention given to the principle of negative resistance we discussed in the Push-up.

Begin by taking a reverse grip on the bar, your hands 12–14 inches apart. Pull yourself up until your chin is over the bar, pause, then let yourself down. The work must be confined strictly to your upper body. If you have to struggle and kick with your feet to finish a rep, then the exercise is no longer effective. Your breathing should be the same in all three variations: Exhale as you pull up; inhale as you return to beginning position.

Perform only the number of reps you can do perfectly. Try to do at least 5.

Rest briefly and then go to the second variation. Grasp the bar with your palms facing toward the front and your hands well beyond shoulder width. To begin, pull your body up until your chin is over the bar. Let yourself down slowly.

Do 5 reps or as many as you can without sacrificing good form. Rest.

Assume the same position as before. This time, pull up so the bar touches in the back of your neck. Some bodybuilders alternate 1 rep to the chin, 1 rep to the back of the neck. I feel this takes away valuable concentration and makes the exercise less effective.

Do 5 reps—more if you can.

NOTE: For all variations of the Chin-up I suggest you begin with 1 set of 5 reps and add reps to a second set until you have 2 sets of 5 reps.

ABDOMINALS

The muscles in the abdominal section are the rectus abdominis and the external obliques. The two exercises I have chosen for this section will help tighten them, compress your waist, and eventually give a nice flat quilted look to your midsection.

The Twisting Sit-up

Begin with your feet held in place—under a bed or heavy chair or secured by the strap on a regular exercise bench—and your knees bent slightly. Clasp your hands behind your back, and as you start to sit up begin twisting from the waist until your right elbow touches your left knee. Alternate on the next rep so your left elbow touches your right knee. Exhale as you sit up; inhale as you return to the floor.

Perform 10 to 20 reps. Try to add a second set of 10 to 20 reps by the third week.

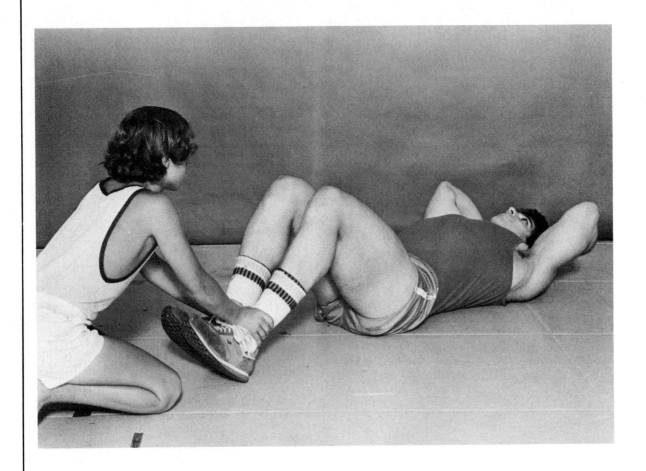

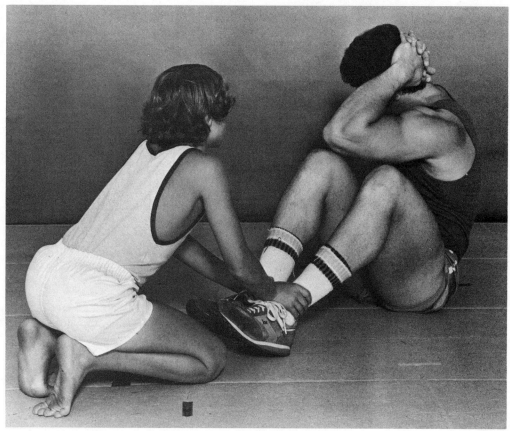

Knees to the Chest

The action of this exercise is like a pump. It works to burn off fat in the lower abdomen.

Lie on your back on a bench or on the floor with your hands under your buttocks. Elevate your legs a couple of inches off the floor and pull your knees into the area of your chest. Push your legs back to the starting position. Exhale as you pull knees to chest; inhale as you thrust them out.

You can do a lot of reps of this exercise in a short time. I suggest beginning with 50 and increasing that to 3 sets of 50 to 60 in three weeks.

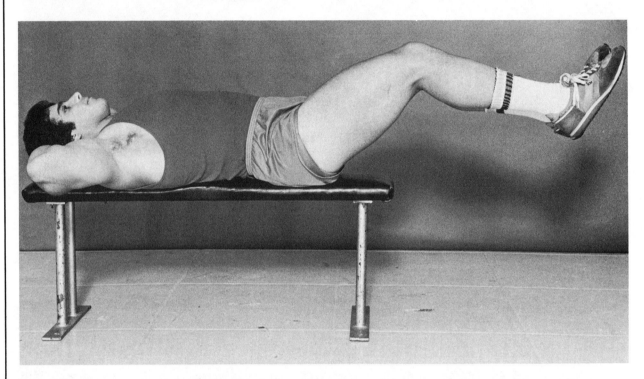

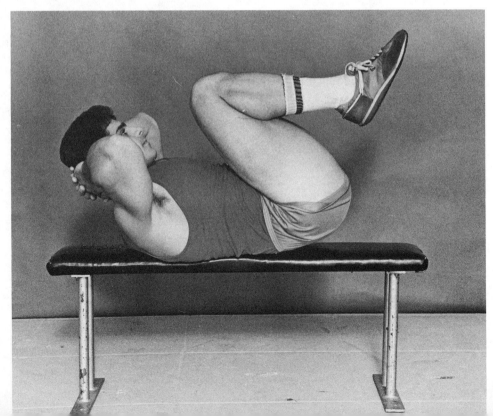

130

BASIC BODYBUILDING

THE GYM

I trained at home for a number of years. It was a convenient and in many ways a satisfying place to work out. But it wasn't until I left my basement gym and went to work out with the pros at R&J Health Club that I really began making great strides in bodybuilding.

A good gym can be many things to a bodybuilder. First and foremost, it is your territory for work and improvement. A gym can provide you with both challenge and gratification; it is a place where new commitments can be made and new horizons realized. The friendships you make in a gym develop in an atmosphere of strength and vitality. Those are positive forces.

Many people have found dramatic changes occurring in their lives after taking up bodybuilding. They have reviewed the rest of their life and found they wanted to cut out activities and even people who were not part of their new and more healthy program and outlook. I consider these changes to be evidence in support of a point I made earlier about how mind, body, and spirit seek a kind of unity which can be encouraged by your efforts in bodybuilding.

CHOOSING A GYM

I train hard to stay in shape for my television and film work as well as for my guest appearances at worldwide bodybuilding events. I work out in two gyms—Gold's Gym and World Gym. They are less than a mile apart, but I find the change of pace, feeling, and general atmosphere to be helpful in sustaining my interest. You will probably find that one gym is sufficient. However, in choosing your gym there are a few points worth discussing.

Both Gold's Gym and World Gym are famous professional establishments dedicated to no-nonsense hard workouts. The equipment is adequate and there is plenty of space. Both gyms are light and well ventilated. They are not oversold in membership, and the people who go to both places are dedicated to the sport. It will be easier for you to get a thorough workout if you are around serious bodybuilders.

Here is a checklist of desirable qualities in a gym:
1. Gym conveniently located.
2. Membership not too large for the facility. Do you see lines waiting for any equipment?
3. Atmosphere right for training.
4. Equipment up-to-date and plentiful.
5. Exercise areas spacious, well lighted, well ventilated.
6. Ample locker space.
7. Clean and adequate showers.

TRAINING PARTNERS

I can understand a person's wanting to train alone. I have done it often, especially when I was young. But I have always noticed a difference in the quality of my workouts when I trained with a partner. There are a number of reasons why a partner can help you. Obligation and incentive are key words here. Once you are committed to a schedule with another person you feel bound to meet at the appointed time, which means you will be less likely to miss workouts. Partners feel the need to help each other's progress, to call for that one last rep or to point out some flaw in form. You can inspire and encourage each other with criticism and praise. You can reinforce each other in moments when you need that extra little push to go beyond a routine performance.

MIRRORS

Most gyms are set up with mirrors in all exercise areas. Learn to use them from the beginning to check your form. By watching yourself, you should be able to tell whether you are doing an exercise properly and how the exercise affects your muscles.

LEGS

Again, we start with your legs. My conviction is that you are only as strong as your legs. To neglect them is like building a house on a weak foundation.

The Squat

Start with your heels on a length of 2×4, your feet 12–14 inches apart; using a barbell with a weight you can handle comfortably, balance it across your shoulders as you see in the photograph. To help maintain your balance, look straight ahead and keep your upper body erect. Inhale as you go down slowly. Stop when your thighs are parallel to the floor. Exhale as you come back up to the beginning position.

Increase the weight as you can. I suggest 2½ pounds per week. Never add so much weight that your back or legs become wobbly. This undermines all progress and could lead to injury.

Begin with 1 set of 10 reps. Increase to 2 sets of 10 to 12 reps.

The Lunge with Barbell

The Lunge with Barbell is terrific for toning up lagging thigh muscles and making them really work. At first glance, this exercise looks like a one-legged Squat, but it requires much more concentrated coordination than the Squat. For this reason it is important to work with a small amount of weight in the beginning and increase the pounds as you can. If you become wobbly during a set because your bar is too heavy, then you are not getting the most out of the Lunges.

Begin by standing with the barbell resting on your shoulders. Take a long step forward with your right leg and allow yourself to go down until your left knee barely touches the floor. Return to the standing position and repeat with the other leg. Keep your movements smooth and controlled. In the second position, both your leg biceps and quadriceps should feel tight; your upper body should be erect and ready to allow you to spring back easily to the beginning position.

Begin with 1 set of 8 reps per leg; increase to 2 sets.

The Bench Press

Possibly the best-known and most popular of all weight-training exercises is the Bench Press. Primarily, the Bench Press affects the pectoral muscles, with some benefit to the front deltoids. It makes a good warm-up for the biceps and triceps exercises to come.

Prepare a barbell on the rack above your exercise bench. Lying on the bench, grasp the bar just beyond shoulder width. Lift the bar from the rack, lock your arms for a moment, then lower the bar slowly until it touches your chest. Press the bar slowly until your arms are locked. Inhale as you lower the bar; exhale as you press the bar. It is important that the Bench Press be smoothly executed; do not bounce or jerk the weight at any point.

Build to 1 set of 10 reps the first week. Increase to 2 sets of 10 reps.

ARMS: BICEPS

Biceps muscles are my favorite body part. I worked hardest on my arms as a young bodybuilder, and my biceps were the first muscles anyone singled out for praise. In the beginning, before I had even achieved any real finish, I was already known for my famous double-arm pose.

The Standing Military Curl

The Standing Military Curl is the best exercise I know to build rock-hard biceps and give them some peak.

To channel all the work to your arms, stand with your feet approximately 16 inches apart and your knees slightly bent. Grip the bar at shoulder width, palms up. Start with the bar against your thighs and curl the bar up to your shoulders. Make certain your back remains straight and move only your forearms. Taking full advantage of negative resistance, lower the bar slowly back to your thighs. Inhale as you curl the bar; exhale as you extend it.

Begin with 1 set of 8 reps.

ARMS: TRICEPS

The triceps, the muscles in the backs of your arms, will already be warmed up from the Standing Military Curl.

The French Press

Either from a standing position or seated on an exercise bench, take a moderate grip on a barbell and raise it above your head. Lower the barbell slowly behind your neck, as you see in the photograph. Raise the weight back to the beginning position. Inhale as you lower the weight; exhale as you push it up. To isolate the triceps, allow only your forearm to move with the barbell.

Perform 1 set of 12 reps. Increase to 2 sets of 10 to 12 reps.

SHOULDERS

Strong, broad shoulders are more than the mark of an athlete. They add to the carriage of any man and make him more impressive.

The Military Press

To develop the deltoid muscles I have always favored the Military Press. It is a barbell exercise that works directly on the deltoids and gives an additional workout to the triceps.

Stand with your feet well apart, your knees and hips locked. Take a wide palms-down grip on the bar and raise it to your chest. Press the barbell overhead, locking your arms. Lower the bar slowly to your chest. Exhale as you press; inhale as you lower the weight. Maintaining proper stance and breathing will help concentrate the work on your deltoids.

Begin with 1 set of 8 reps. Increase to 2 sets of 8 reps.

BACK: LATISSIMUS DORSI

Huge lats give you the broad, V-shaped back that adds a look of power to your overall physique.

Bent-Over Rowing

To give maximum spread and size to the lats there is no finer exercise than Bent-Over Rowing.

Stand with your feet spread 12–14 inches for support and your knees slightly bent. Bend forward until your upper body is parallel to the floor. Grip the bar with palms down just under your shoulders. Keep your back flat and pull the bar to your chest. Hold to the count of two and lower the bar slowly to beginning position. Exhale as you lift; inhale as you lower the bar. I find that it helps get the full movement of Bent-Over Rowing if I stand on a sturdy exercise block as shown in the photograph.

Do 1 set of 10 reps. Increase to 2 sets of 10 reps.

143

Fabulous heart-shaped calves are the mark of finish in a conscientious bodybuilder. Your calf muscles have been worked since the day you began walking. They can take plenty of weight. But more important than the number of pounds is how you exercise the calves. They need the absolute full range of possible movement—both in extension (or stretch) and contraction.

Standing Calf Raise on a Machine

Position yourself on the calf machine, with your toes on a high block. Lift your entire body against the bars of the machine, going up to the absolute maximum. Hold that briefly, then lower your body, allowing your heels to go down as far as possible. Pause and let the calf muscles really stretch. Repeat.

Perform 1 set of 15 reps. Increase to 2 sets of 15 reps.

The Twisting Sit-up (Bent Knees)

Begin with your feet held in place—under a bed or a heavy chair or secured by your training partner or by the strap on a regular exercise bench—and your knees bent at approximately a 45-degree angle. Clasp your hands behind your back, and as you start to sit up begin twisting from the waist until your right elbow touches your left knee. Alter-nate on the next rep so your left elbow touches your right knee. Exhale as you sit up; inhale as you return to the floor.

1 set of 50 reps. Increase to 2 sets of 50 reps.

The Leg Raise

The Twisting Sit-up was primarily to exercise the upper abdominals and obliques. Leg Raises will burn the fat from your lower abs and help create the hard, studded look a bodybuilder wants to have through his entire abdominal section.

Lying on an exercise bench with your legs extended over the end and your knees bent (this helps prevent straining your lower back as well as concentrating the effort to your abs), bring your legs up until you feel your abs contract. Lower your legs and repeat, keeping a smooth steady rhythm to both the up and down movements. You will notice in the photograph that my eyes are fo- cused on my abs. This is not only for concentration but to put an additional contraction into the area of my upper abs and allow me to benefit there.

Begin with 1 set of 20 reps. Increase to 2 sets of 30 reps.

RULES AND REMINDERS

1. Exercise only three days a week at this stage of training, with a rest day between each workout day for rest and recuperation.
2. Remember to pay attention to correct form. Do not sacrifice form for either added weight or more reps.
3. Always concentrate on the exercise, not on what is going on in the gym. Give your time to working out, not to horsing around.
4. Add weight gradually and in a logical way. I suggest a 2½-to-5 pound increase per week.

BASIC BODYBUILDING TRAINING SCHEDULE

Increase weight weekly—2½ to 5 pounds—but do not put on more than you can handle with proper form while maintaining the following schedule.

EXERCISE	STAGE ONE	STAGE TWO	STAGE THREE
Squat	Build to 2 sets of 10–12 reps.	Build to 3 sets of 12 reps.	Build to 4 sets of 15 reps.
Lunge	Build to 2 sets of 8 reps per leg.	Build to 3 sets of 8–10 reps per leg.	Build to 4 sets of 10 reps per leg.
Bench Press	Build to 2 sets of 10 reps.	Build to 3 sets of 10–12 reps.	Build to 4 sets of 10–12 reps.
Military Curl	Build to 2 sets of 8–10 reps.	Build to 3 sets of 10 reps.	Build to 4 sets of 10 reps.
French Press	Build to 2 sets of 10–12 reps.	Build to 3 sets of 10 reps.	Build to 4 sets of 10 reps.
Military Press	Build to 2 sets of 8 reps.	Build to 3 sets of 8–10 reps.	Build to 4 sets of 8–10 reps.
Bent-Over Rowing	Build to 2 sets of 10 reps.	Build to 3 sets of 10 reps.	Build to 4 sets of 10 reps.
Calf Raise	Build to 2 sets of 15 reps.	Build to 3 sets of 15–20 reps.	Build to 4 sets of 20 reps.
Sit-up	Build to 2 sets of 50 reps.	Build to 3 sets of 50–70 reps.	Build to 4 sets of 60 reps.
Leg Raise	Build to 2 sets of 30 reps.	Build to 3 sets of 30–40 reps.	Build to 4 sets of 30–40 reps.

Note: Continue the basic bodybuilding exercises at least four months, adding reps and weight as your body can handle the increases. If you do not feel you have thoroughly mastered these exercises by that time, continue this program for the fifth or sixth month before moving on to the advanced course.

ADVANCED BODYBUILDING

You have now completed your basic bodybuilding training under my guidance. This is a crucial time for you as a bodybuilder. You will now have reached a natural plateau at which you have already achieved all your easiest and most obvious goals. A quick review of your training notebook will tell you how dramatically your body has changed. By sticking out the months of basic bodybuilding you have demonstrated your strong determination and your dedication to superior strength and good health.

These are important qualities to have in order to proceed to the advanced bodybuilding course. From now on the obvious gains will be smaller and visible changes will come more slowly. They must be measured now in muscle quality rather than in muscle size. There will be familiar exercises from the basic course—some bodybuilding exercises cannot be improved upon—but there will also be new exercises which work the muscles in a different way in order to reach down into hard-to-get-at areas.

In many ways the advanced course is dedicated to refinement. And that takes time and patience.

A NEW ASSESSMENT

It is time to start a new notebook, time to reassess your aims and goals. I am certain you were surprised at the radical changes in thinking you experienced during the basic bodybuilding course. Your ideas about yourself, about bodybuilding, and about the people around you may have changed more than at any other brief period in your life. This is not uncommon when you are engaging in a new activity that has as much impact as bodybuilding. I suggest that you use the beginning and end photos from the basic course diary as the first page of your advanced training diary.

MENTAL ATTITUDE AND GOALS

I like to think of the mind as the strongest muscle in the body. Once your mind is made up and you have zeroed in on your goals and shut out all negative possibilities, you are on the road to success.

Strong belief is the prime motivator for goal achievement. You know this from the successful visualization you experienced in the beginning courses. Your mind has an odd ability to ignore differences between present and future. Once you have fixed a certain image in your mind and you believe in it strongly, your mind sees it not as something in the future but as an accomplished fact. It is important to utilize this principle in the advanced bodybuilding course. You must visualize in precise detail all your goals, large and small, and see each minute change in your body.

The difference between your bodybuilding efforts in the past few months and what you will be doing ahead is like the difference between being a mechanic and a jeweler. The waist size you wanted eight months ago is now a reality. You have developed your arms, legs, chest, and back. From this point on you will also be working to bring out the smaller, more detailed areas such as the serratus magnus and the fingerlike attachments of the latissimus dorsi.

MUSCLE PRIORITY TRAINING

The more you work a muscle, the faster it grows and improves. However, this growth and development is relative to each individual bodybuilder and even to individual muscles within each body. Many bodybuilders find that their legs refuse to respond as readily as their arms or that their calves don't seem to grow; often one biceps will outmeasure the other by as much as an inch. The only way to correct these imbalances is to bombard the lagging muscles with work and bring them up to size. This is called *muscle priority training.*

The best time to hit these slow-to-develop muscles is when you are fresh, during the first few minutes of a workout. Then you can bring to focus all your energy and concentration and really blast the muscle. Even the most stubborn muscle will respond to this kind of attention.

LIFTING BELTS

You have heard the old adage "Prevention is the best cure." Nowhere does it make more sense than in heavy-duty training, where you are constantly taking your body to the limit. It is of prime importance to your continual progress that you do everything to avoid injury. Sensible training techniques are your key to protection:

1. Warm up thoroughly before every training session.
2. Train within your known personal limits.

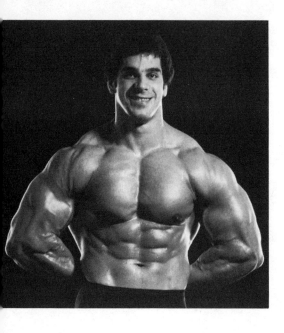

3. Never add more weight than you can handle in good form.
4. Practice the breathing techniques I have given with each exercise.

For many people the lower back becomes a problem in heavy lifting. Even if they employ good biomechanical positions they are prone to back injury. To prevent this in my own workouts for back and legs and for strenuous overhead pressing movements I protect myself with a 6-inch-wide leather lifting belt. These belts are available in professional gyms or by mail order. I suggest you consider using one during your rigorous back and leg training.

TRAINING TO FAILURE AND CHEATING

After six to nine months of conscientious weight training your body should be strong enough to be pushed—if you are serious about training to the limit and wish to do so. Two of the techniques used by the pros to get an extra burn into the muscle and promote even greater growth are *training to failure* and *cheating*.

Training to failure means continuing the reps of an exercise set until you absolutely cannot complete a repetition and still maintain the prescribed form—that is, your arms refuse to lift the bar, or your calves cannot push you back to the top. A few weeks before an important contest the top bodybuilders will be taking almost every set to failure—and even beyond.

What is beyond failure? We call it cheating. Though it is not desirable to cheat during the basic course, it has its advantages as a training tool for advanced bodybuilders. As a beginning bodybuilder you are likely to cheat in order to take stress away from a muscle—in other words, to make the work easier. At this point, cheating is a technique to *add* stress to a muscle.

It works this way. Once you have taken a set to failure—which means you have been physically unable to complete that last rep—you cheat to push yourself past the point at which the muscles seem to stick. Let's say you can't make the last few inches of a Wide-Grip Chin so you give a kick with your feet to get you beyond that difficult inch or so. From then on you should resume strict form. This will be painful. But that pain is essential to ultimate muscle size and definition.

SETS AND REPS

In the advanced bodybuilding course you will need to make decisions about numbers of sets and reps and the amount of weight you will be lifting. Many of these decisions will depend on your goals—contest training or superior fitness. Never push your body so far as to suffer an injury. The best rule to prevent injury is to use only as much weight as you can while maintaining proper form.

At this stage in the development of your physique, the muscle groups require more concentrated attention in order to continue growing. By splitting the body into two logically chosen groups of body parts and training them on alternate days with spaced rest days in between, you will be able to give individual muscles a complete workout and then sufficient rest for complete recuperation.

Notice that I have included calf and abdominal exercises for every day you are in the gym. These two areas always need work and do not require the recuperation time most of the other muscles need.

MONDAY AND THURSDAY EXERCISES

On these days you will work legs, chest, lower back, calves, and abdominals.

LEGS

You know my feeling that the legs are the foundation of a great body. In order fully to realize the potential of your leg muscles you need to give careful attention to each muscle in this group. The leg biceps is as important as the quadriceps; especially important is striking a good balance between upper thigh work and work around the lower thigh and the knee. Because the legs contain large masses of muscle it is possible to overwork them. My advice is to work heavy—especially thigh exercises—using fewer reps and sets and more weight to avoid becoming exhausted. Exhaustion is counterproductive.

The Squat

You are familiar with the basic movements of the Squat. It is my favorite leg exercise, the exercise I would choose if I could only do one.

I am introducing a variation of the Squat, the Hack Squat, now because after nine months you will have the strength and co-ordination to perform it properly. The Front Squat is as effective as the Squat, with the advantages of isolating the quadriceps better and putting less stress on the hips and lower back. This means you can work with more weight.

I suggest you warm up with the Squat, then move to the Front Squat and the Hack Squat to begin really bombing your legs.

The basic movements and rules we have discussed in the Squat apply to the variations. The main difference is the positioning of the weight; this is illustrated in the following photographs.

The Hack Squat on a Machine

The Hack Squat Machine helps isolate the lower part of the quadriceps that usually don't get much of a workout.

Position yourself on the machine with your legs slightly unlocked. Release the weight and lower yourself slowly until your leg biceps are against your calves. Without allowing your back to move away from the backrest, press your body to the top. By never locking your knees at the beginning or end of a rep, you keep your thigh muscles under constant tension throughout the set.

Build to 4 sets of 10 to 12 reps.

The Front Squat

Begin with your heels on a 2×4 block. Cross your forearms to grip the bar. Lift the bar and hold it against your chest, as you see me doing in the photograph. Perform the Squat in the normal fashion. By having the weight a few inches ahead of its normal position, the emphasis of the exercise goes to a different area of your thigh muscles and helps you grow and gain definition.

Build to 4 sets of 10 to 12 reps.

The Leg Extension

The Leg Extension will especially affect the rectus femoris, which forms the center of the thigh. It can be fully flexed only by using the Leg Extension machine. With adequate weight and slow, deliberate movement this exercise works the legs as the Curl works the arms.

Sit on the end of the bench with the backs of your knees against the padded edge, as shown in the photograph, and hook your feet under the bar. With a smooth motion, lift the weight until your legs are locked out straight. Hold this position briefly and slowly lower the bar to the beginning position. Always extend your legs fully and hold that extreme position for a count of two before allowing the weight to pull your legs back down.

Build to 4 sets of 10 to 12 reps.

The Leg Curl

The Leg Curl is a refinement exercise. It brings into balance the quadriceps and the leg biceps.

To perform this exercise properly, lie on the Leg Curl machine with your upper body supported on your elbows. This arches your back and helps isolate the leg biceps muscles. Throughout the movement of the exercise, keep your hips flat on the bench. Using only your leg biceps, pull the weight up as far as you can toward your buttocks, hold for a count of two, then lower it to the fully extended position.

Build to 5 sets of 10 to 12 reps.

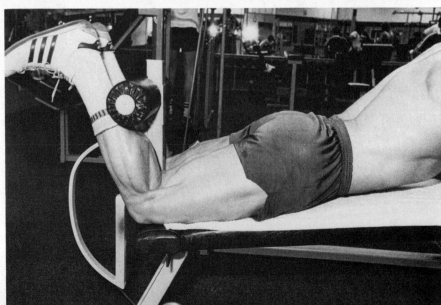

CHEST

A powerful, well-muscled chest not only ties in the development of the arms and shoulders to the rest of the upper torso and offsets a strong back, it also provides protection for such vital organs as the heart and lungs.

The Bench Press

The Bench Press with a barbell, which is the pectoral exercise you have done to this point, should be your warm-up exercise for the chest.

The Incline Bench Press

A shift in body position changes the effect of an exercise. The Incline Bench Press takes the work to the middle and upper areas of the pectoral muscles.

Take hold of the bar in the same manner you would grip it for the regular Bench Press. Hold it above your chest, arms extended, and lower it slowly until it touches your chest. Lift it back to the starting position and repeat. After a few reps you will begin to feel the difference between this and the regular Bench Press.

Build to 4 sets of 8 to 10 reps.

The Dumbbell Incline Press

To bring a slightly different focus to the pectorals I suggest you move next to the Dumbbell Incline Press. See the photographs for grip and positioning information.

Start with the dumbbells a few inches apart above your chest. Lower them slowly, allowing the pectorals to get a full stretch, pause, then press them back to the top. One important note: Do not try to handle the same weight you use for the Bench Press. Without the stability of the bar it is impossible. However, the coordination called for in keeping the dumbbells moving smoothly makes up for this drop in poundage.

Build to 10 sets of 10 to 12 reps.

Dumbbell Flyes

Dumbbell Flyes exercise every area of the pectorals. By varying the bench positions—incline, flat, decline—you can direct the work to every area of your chest.

Holding the dumbbells above the chest, with your elbows only slightly bent (a position they must keep throughout the exercise), slowly swing the dumbbells out and down until you reach the extreme position. Stretch the pectorals, then bring the dumbbells slowly and smoothly back to the beginning position. Constant tension and a complete stretch in the pectoral muscles will ensure the maximum benefit from the Flyes.

Build to 4 sets of 8 to 10 reps.

The Decline Bench Press

Because of the shift in the position of your body when the lower end of the exercise bench is elevated, the movements of the Decline Bench Press direct the work of this exercise to your lower and outer pectoral muscles, areas which are too often neglected.

The bench should be set at approximately 45 degrees. Grip the bar as you would for the regular flat Bench Press. Lower the bar slowly until it just touches your neck. (This is an obvious example of a time when your training partner is absolutely essential!) Inhale as you lower the weight; exhale as you press it back to the top.

Build to 4 sets of 8 to 12 reps.

LOWER BACK

The lower back is often neglected, since it is perhaps the least showy of all the areas of the body. This is a serious mistake in advanced training because a strong, supple lower back is the necessary link to all the great power movements. Combine the following exercises with Barbell Rowing for a complete program.

The Good-Morning Exercise with a Barbell

Start this exercise with a light weight for a good warm-up and then add pounds to the bar as you go. Begin with your feet about shoulder width, the **barbell** resting on your shoulders, and your back slightly arched. *Under no circumstances should you allow your back to round during any movement of the Good-Morning.* Bend forward as far as you can and still maintain the slight arch to your

back. Go no farther. Return slowly to the standing position. Note that in the photograph of the extreme stretched position my knees are slightly bent. This allows the hamstrings to get a good workout along with the lower back.

Build to 4 sets of 8 to 10 reps.

Hyperextensions

Hyperextensions go directly to the spinae erectors.

Position yourself on the bench, your thighs on the
bench, your heels locked securely under the bars,
and your hands clasped behind your head. Starting from the bottom position, raise your body
slowly to the extended position.

Do not allow your back to arch any more than
mine is arched; a greater arch could compress the
discs in your back and cause discomfort. I try for
15 reps. If I go beyond 15, I often hold a barbell
plate behind my neck for added resistance.

Build to 4 sets of 10 to 12 reps.

CALVES

The calves need work every day you are in the gym. Only through constant effort can they be brought up to the level of development of the rest of your body. You are familiar with Standing Calf Raises. I want to add another exercise.

Seated Calf Raise on a Machine

The soleus is a very strong, difficult-to-hit muscle placed directly beneath the calf (gastrocnemius). The Seated Calf Raise is vital to getting at the soleus.

Seated on the calf machine with your knees fully under the bar and your toes on the block, lift until the calf is completely flexed, hold for a count of two, then slowly stretch the calf, bringing your heels down as far as possible. In this exercise it is important never to bounce in either extreme position.

Build to 4 sets of 12 to 15 reps.

Donkey Calf Raise

Donkey Calf Raises work the entire calf as well as giving a thorough stretch to the hamstrings. In order to keep the work primarily in the calf muscles I suggest performing this exercise with your knees slightly unlocked.

Assume a bent-over position, bracing your hands on a high bench such as a leg machine, and have your training partner climb on your back and position himself as far down on your hips as possible. Then step up on the calf block and proceed as you would in any calf exercise. Always go as far up on your toes as you can and then slowly let your heels down to get a full, long stretch.

Build to 4 sets of 15 to 20 reps.

ABDOMINALS

A finely quilted abdominal area is one of the marks of a finished physique. Like the calves, the abs require constant attention. When working for contest-quality definition it is essential to combine abdominal work with a stringent diet. Even the slightest amount of fat over this region can obscure these muscles. For the Monday-and-Thursday program I am suggesting two abdominal exercises.

The Abdominal Crunch

The Abdominal Crunch is the prime exercise for isolating the upper abdominals.

Begin with your feet elevated and your knees bent, your back flat and your hands clasped behind your head. Having your legs in this position restricts the work to the abs. Draw your head toward your knees until you feel the abdominal muscles crunch together. The movement is relatively slight. The important thing is the tightening of the muscles. Hold the extreme position for a count of two and slowly return to the start.

Build to 4 sets of 25 to 30 reps.

The Vertical Pulley Crunch

The Vertical Pulley Crunch is a special exercise to isolate the serratus and intercostal muscles and give a look of finish to your whole midsection.

Using the high pulley station on the pulley machine, attach the rope handle to the cable end in order to have some flexibility in the extreme positions of the Pulley Crunch. To begin, get on your knees facing the pulley machine, keeping your buttocks well above your heels, and grasp the rope attachment with both hands. As you will note by inspecting both photographs, there is no change in the position of my legs and my arms move very little during the movements of this exercise. It is essential to use your abdominal muscles to pull the weight. Not only is the Pulley Crunch effective but the extreme stretch also works the entire area.

Build to 4 sets of 25 to 30 reps.

The Leg Raise on a Flat Bench

The Leg Raise directs the work to your lower abdominal muscles.

Lie on a bench with your legs bent slightly and your chin tucked into your chest. Lift your legs as high as you can, hold for a count of two, and lower them back to the beginning position. The reason for doing this on a bench is to keep your legs from touching the floor and thus to maintain a constant tension in the lower abdominals. The Leg Raises can be done with slightly more speed than the Crunches. However, after a good workout both exercises should give a hard burning sensation in the abs.

Build to 4 sets of 25 to 30 reps.

TUESDAY AND FRIDAY EXERCISES

On these days you will work the arms, shoulders, back, calves, and abdominals.

Some bodybuilders fail to recognize how important it is to maintain a perfect balance between muscle groups. This is nowhere more noticeable than between the quadriceps and the biceps in the legs or the biceps and the triceps in the arms.

ARMS: BICEPS

Warm up the biceps with the Standing Military Curl, the biceps exercise you have done for a number of months.

The Incline Curl

Sit on an incline bench set at approximately 45 degrees. Begin with the dumbbells in the lower position, your palms facing each other, and as you lift gradually rotate them until in the extreme top position your palms are facing your shoulders. This may sound more difficult than it is. Study the photograph carefully for the proper movement. During this exercise keep your chin slightly tucked and your eyes straight ahead. The rotating motion brings work into the lower biceps area, and a hard flex at the top directs it into the biceps peak. Always hold the extreme top position briefly and concentrate on the peak. This added attention from your mind adds that extra growth you need at this point.

Build to 4 sets of 8 to 10 reps.

ARMS: TRICEPS

The triceps are really beautifully detailed muscles in the backs of your arms. Because they make up over two-thirds of the upper arm, failure to develop them costs inches in overall arm measurement. The Triceps Extension from the beginning bodybuilding course will warm up all three heads of this impressive muscle group. Then move to the following exercises.

The Lying Triceps Press

Lie on a flat exercise bench with your feet braced on the bench and your head just off the end of the bench. Grip a barbell at slightly closer than shoulder width and hold it directly above your chest. This is the starting position. Now, keeping your back flat against the bench, lower the bar behind your head, extending it as far as you can. Lift it slowly back to the starting position. Throughout the entire range of movement, try to maintain a constant tension in the triceps.

Build to 4 sets of 10 to 12 reps.

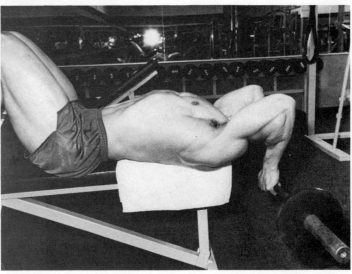

The Triceps Press-down

The Triceps Press-down, which makes use of the overhead pulley machine, keeps a continuous tension on the entire triceps muscle group. Grasp the bar with your palms down and your hands spread approximately 4 inches apart. Throughout the exercise, your upper arms should be pressed tightly against the sides of your rib cage (see photo-graph). Press the bar down until your arms are fully extended, then cramp your triceps. To do this, move your hands as if you were trying to bend the bar. This puts the final effort into the triceps where you want it.

Build to 4 sets of 10 to 12 reps.

The Triceps Cable Kickback

The Triceps Cable Kickback gives finish and detailing to the three heads of your triceps. It requires only a moderate range of movement, but it adds that extra bit of work to bring out real muscle quality.

Facing the low pulley station of the pulley machine, grasp the handle and bend over so the line of your back is parallel to the floor and the cable handle is close to your thigh. Push the handle back as you see in the photograph to contract your triceps. Slowly allow your hand to return to the starting position. The movements of this exercise should be evenly spaced and strict, with a brief pause in the extreme position to ensure a complete flexing of the triceps. Perform a complete set with one arm before going to the other arm.

Build to 4 sets of 8 to 10 reps.

FOREARMS

Your forearms take a certain amount of work from many other exercises. However, when you reach the stage of advanced bodybuilding you need to concentrate on forearm development through specific forearm exercises.

The Reverse Curl

Take a fairly narrow (10-12-inch) grip on the barbell with your palms down. Begin with the barbell against your thighs and your upper arms stationary against your rib cage. Using your forearms only, lift the bar as high as you can, pause, then lower it slowly to the starting position. Both movements of the Reverse Curl benefit the forearm.

Build to 5 sets of 12 to 15 reps.

The Wrist Curl

With the Reverse Curl as an effective warm-up exercise, the Wrist Curl goes directly to the belly of the forearm to give it the greatest possible size.

Grasp the barbell with your palms facing up and your hands no more than 4 inches apart. Sit on a bench, your legs spread, your forearms between them, and your wrists barely over the end. Begin with the bar loosely held in your fingers and your wrists extended as far down as they will go. Tighten your grip slightly on the bar and lift it until your forearms are fully contracted. Hold this position briefly, then return slowly to the beginning position. This exercise may also be performed with your palms down, as in the pictures below, to give your forearms a double workout.

Build to 5 sets of 12 to 15 reps.

SHOULDERS

Broad shoulders have always been the image of manly strength. They suggest both power and endurance and the ability to forge ahead. In bodybuilding they are important to defining the physique and tying in the entire upper torso. The deltoids have three heads, of which the frontal head is usually overdeveloped from too much chest work and the rear head is neglected. Again, this brings me back to my insistence on balance between the muscles within each group. The familiar Military Press will be a good beginning for the deltoid work.

Upright Barbell Rowing

To get at the front deltoid I like Upright Barbell Rowing, which is an exercise not used by a great number of bodybuilders. One advantage to Upright Barbell Rowing is that it also reaches the trapezius and in this way helps tie shoulders and back together.

Stand with your feet slightly apart for good balance and take a narrow grip on the bar, your palms facing your body. Begin with the bar touching your thighs and your arms fully extended, bring the bar up, keeping it close to your body (as in the first photograph), and try to get it to eye level. Lower the bar slowly back until your arms are fully extended. It is important to draw the weight up slowly and not to cheat by swinging it away from your body. If you feel this happening it is a sure indication that you are trying to lift too much weight.

Build to 4 sets of 8 to 10 reps.

Side Lateral Raise

The Side Lateral Raise specifically works the lateral head of the deltoid, the development of which gives your shoulders their width.

To begin, hold two dumbbells in front of your thighs, your palms facing each other. Stand bent forward slightly to isolate the lateral deltoids with your elbows barely unlocked. Then as you lift your arms rotate your wrists just slightly so your little finger ends up higher than your forefinger. Lower the weights slowly to the beginning position and repeat.

Build to 4 sets of 10 to 12 reps.

Side Lateral Raise with a Pulley

To give a variation on this exercise I am including the following photographs to illustrate the Side Lateral Raise with a pulley.

The movements are basically the same, except you work first one arm and then the other. By grasping the machine and gaining that stability you will be able to handle more weight and really get to the lateral head of your delts.

Build to 4 sets of 10 to 12 reps.

Bent-Over Lateral Raise

To take care of the rear deltoids the Bent-Over Lateral Raise is one of the most effective exercises.

Position yourself between two pulleys or use two dumbbells, as you see in the photograph. You should be bent over at the waist, looking directly ahead, with your feet well spread and your knees bent slightly. Grasp the dumbbells or the handles on the cables and raise your arms until they are approximately parallel to the floor and, if you are using the pulleys, the cables are crossed in front of your legs. Return slowly to the beginning position. The negative resistance is almost as beneficial as lifting the weight.

Build to 4 sets of 8 to 10 reps.

BACK

Along with stunning abdominals a completely developed back becomes the concern of any bodybuilder moving beyond the beginning stages. The various positions of the Chin-up as well as Bent-Over Rowing have given you the foundation for a powerful back. Use them to warm up the entire latissimus dorsi and then move on to the new exercises in this section.

The Pull-down on the Lat Machine

Building wide lats with a definite V configuration requires the heavy vertical pulling movements the lat machine was engineered to provide.

Seat yourself securely under the T-bar so you can concentrate your total effort on the pull-down and grasp the bar a few inches wider apart than your shoulders. The starting position should give you a complete stretch. There should be enough weight on the pulley to give your shoulder blades the sensation of being pulled apart. Pull the bar straight down and try to touch your chest with it. At that point you should feel that your lats are fully contracted. Working against the weight, return the bar to the full stretch, pause, and begin your second rep.

Build to 4 sets of 8 to 10 reps.

The Lat Pull-down Behind the Neck

A highly effective variation on the previous exercise is the Lat Pull-down Behind the Neck.

In the same position on the lat machine, but with a slightly wider grip on the bar, I pull it down and touch the back of my neck, as seen in the photographs. Here too it is important to return the bar to the stretch position as slowly as possible and still maintain a good rhythm.

Build to 4 sets of 8 to 10 reps.

CALVES

Because you have done no leg work at all on the Tuesday-and-Friday program, you should be able to really blast the calf muscles with some heavy sets. As an alternate, I suggest that you begin your calf work on these days with the Seated Calf Raises and then go to the Standing Calf Raise machine and put in a thorough workout.

Build to 4 sets of 12 to 15 reps.

ABDOMINALS

Begin your abdominal workout with Leg Raises on a Flat Bench. Move to Abdominal Crunches for a hard, burning workout. Finish with an energetic session of bringing knees to chest.

Leg Raises: Build to 4 sets of 25 to 50 reps.
Abdominal Crunches: Build to 4 sets of 25 to 30 reps.
Knees to Chest: Build to 2 sets of 50 reps.

5

SPECIAL BODYBUILDING FOR TEENAGERS

THE FOUNDATION

As you probably know after reading about my life in the first part of this book, I had my share of the problems common among teenage bodybuilders. I spent years training without proper guidance, bombing my arms with heavy work and neglecting other, less showy areas of my body. However, what I learned through trial and error, mistake and success, should be valuable in helping you to avoid those same pitfalls and setbacks.

In the beginning, two general rules should apply to your training with weights:

1. Allow yourself plenty of time to develop your muscles fully.
2. Be patient, stay with the program, and don't try to push too far too fast.

Remember, baseball-hard biceps with the kind of peak mine have will not pop out after your first day with weights, and a lean, muscle-studded stomach takes longer to develop than a mere few weeks of work. You need to tell yourself from the beginning that you are bodybuilding because it is a great sport, that the workouts and the discipline make you feel good, and that you expect results in terms of visible muscle development in a few months, not a few days. Now you are being realistic. After all, one of the most fantastic things about bodybuilding is the incredible feeling of exhilaration it gives you, and you *can* get that your very first session with weights.

Once you have decided that you can wait for the kind of results that can be measured with a tape and have begun to concentrate on the more immediate benefits of training, you have made a giant step in bodybuilding: You have begun to take control of your mind. When you take that step and become master of your mind—your greatest single source of strength—you are already on the road to success with your body. Let me remind you before you go any further that if you have not read the sections of the book that deal with the mental aspects of training, or if you have

182

read them but they still seem unclear, go back and read them carefully, especially Chapter One in Part Two.

A WORD OF CAUTION

Your primary aim in using my course is to build your body; therefore, every bit of effort you make during training sessions should be directed toward that end. Look at it this way: If you were building a house you would begin with a solid foundation and then work brick by brick until you had reached the dimensions set out in your blueprint. Bodybuilding should be the same. Lay a firm foundation and then proceed slowly and steadily until you reach your goal. If you attempt to do too much or go too fast you may become sloppy and actually retard your progress.

The greatest weakness many young bodybuilders have is wanting to start out lifting too much weight. My major concern at this point is to convince you that it is much better to work with a weight that seems comfortable and then to increase the poundage gradually as you fully understand the movements of each exercise. Remember this: Bodybuilding is not a contest of how much weight you can lift. The results you are interested in are a fabulous, well-proportioned body that is both healthy and flexible. So lighten up and let yourself grow.

CORRECT FORM

Your muscles will develop, grow, and harden according to the effectiveness of the work you give them. To achieve the highest

degree of effective work-to-growth benefits you must be aware of the correct form of every exercise. *Do not take shortcuts!* Read each exercise description carefully and go through the movements slowly and completely with a very light bar, dumbbell, or resistance machine until you have memorized the form. Whatever differences the great bodybuilders of the world have in our personal training programs, all of us, including Arnold Schwarzenegger, Franco Columbu, and Frank Zane, are advocates of strict form. If it has worked for us it should work for you. Here, then, is the correct way to learn an exercise: Read the description carefully, go through it slowly using only a light weight, memorize the movements, then start to work on your body.

EATING HABITS

I do not have to tell you how bad your eating habits are. You have heard it from your mother, your teachers, and almost everyone else. What I will say is simple and to the point: Anyone interested in serious bodybuilding sooner or later has to begin eating the kind of foods that produce great muscles. Most diets are adequate in this area but they contain too many sweets, too much fat, too much salt, and too many of the wrong kind of carbohydrates. Cut down in these areas, outlined earlier in the book, and your hours of training will give you better results much faster.

WORKOUTS AT HOME

I have designed this special teenage bodybuilding course to be done at home. The reasons are economics and convenience. There is no need to purchase an expensive gym membership until you are a few years older and into the more advanced stages of bodybuilding that require complex machines and a greater variety of weights. Until I was well into contest training I worked out in my basement gym at home.

The exercises I have selected for the teenage course call for a bare minimum of equipment—one barbell, a few plates, a single exercise bench, and a pair of dumbbells. These are carried in the sporting-goods departments of most major stores or can be ordered by mail from any of the top muscle magazines.

Training at home has the added advantage of making it possible for you to work out with a good friend or, as I often did, with your father. Working together and growing together is great for a relationship—whether it is a friend, brother, or father. It helps keep the edge on your enthusiasm and gives you a chance to inspire another person and be inspired by their example.

WARM-UP

I never begin to train without a thorough warm-up. The purpose of this warm-up session is to prepare my muscles for the hard workout ahead. It has the same beneficial results as warming up a car engine on a cold morning: better performance, more efficiency, less chance of problems later on. I start slowly and go through a series of simple, freehand exercise movements that reach deep into each muscle. All of these movements constitute a complete stretch, which allows the blood to flow freely to the tissue and in turn promotes growth.

For your body, the teenage body, which is still growing and filling out, the short warm-up period is especially important. No matter how impatient you are to get to the weight rack and start hard training, you should always take time to warm-up. Aside from just warming your muscles, those few minutes will help you build up the discipline you need to continue with serious body-building.

During my own warm-up I am also working on my mind. I think through the entire workout I have planned for that day. I psych myself up for the successes I am going to have, and I know then how great I will feel when I am finished and in the shower.

The movements given below are only a few of the many stretching exercises you can do. However, they work together to give your body a complete pretraining stretch, and I suggest that you stick with them throughout the teenage program.

The Full-Body Stretch

Stand with your feet a few inches apart and reach as high as you can over your head. In the extreme position you should be on tiptoe and feel your entire body extended and tingling slightly. Repeat twice more.

Back Bow

This is similar to the first stretch except that you keep your feet flat on the floor and reach over your head and back as far as you can while still maintaining perfect balance. It is important to make a nice bow of your body and stretch back until you feel it in all the muscles of your front body—thighs, abs, pecs, delts, neck. Repeat twice more.

Toe Touch

Reach down slowly—keeping your legs straight and firmly planted—and touch the floor, first with the tips of your fingers, then your knuckles, and finally your hands. Go only as far down in the be- ginning as you can and work up to the extreme position during the next few days. Remember to go through all the movements smoothly and *without bouncing.* Repeat twice more.

Side Bends

Start with your feet spread approximately 18 inches apart and your left arm against your left leg. Reach over your head with your right hand and bend to the left until you have slid your left hand down to your ankle. Repeat these same movements to the right side. Repeat entire exercise twice.

Stretch to Alternate Toes

Standing with your feet 20–24 inches apart, reach with both hands and touch the toes of your right foot. You should keep both knees straight and try to move as far to the side as possible. Return to the upright position and touch both hands to your left toes. Repeat twice more to each side.

Pelvic Lift

Lie on your back with your knees bent and your hands clasped behind your neck. Lift your buttocks as high off the floor as you can and hold yourself in that position for a few seconds. Lower your body slowly to the floor. Repeat twice more.

Seated Toe Touch

Sit on the floor with your legs together and extended in front of you. Without allowing your knees to bend, reach and touch your toes. Continue to come as far forward as you can with your upper body. Your goal should be to touch your forehead to your legs. Repeat twice more.

188

Knees to Chest

Lying on your back on the floor, draw your right knee up until you can clasp it with both hands (as you see in the photograph). Pull your thigh against your chest and gradually bring your head up to touch your knee. Do the same movements with the left leg. Then perform the complete exercise with both legs at the same time.

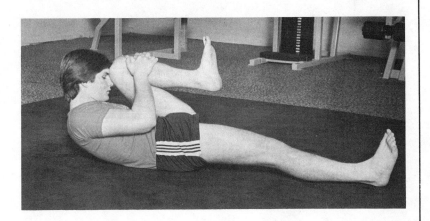

PRETRAINING TONE-UP

Now that your body is stretched out and limber, perform the following toning exercises as a direct lead into your daily work with the weights.

Start with a series of 10 to 20 Bent-Knee Leg Raises. Lie on your back on the floor or on an exercise bench with your palms flat on the floor under your buttocks, then bend your knees slightly and tuck your chin into your chest. Moving only at the hips, bring your legs up as high as you can, then lower them slowly to a point approximately an inch from the floor. Repeat until you have completed your set. Exhale as you lift your legs, inhale as you lower them.

Without a pause, turn onto your stomach for Push-ups. Begin by positioning your hands on the floor under you at the shoulder width. Then, keeping your back perfectly straight, push your body

up until your arms are locked. Now lower your body until you barely touch your chest to the floor, pause, and push your body up until your arms are locked. Repeat 8 to 10 times.

Go directly to the chinning bar. Grip the bar with your palms facing away from your body and at a width a few inches wider than your shoulders. Pull up slowly, using only your arms, until your chin is over the bar, then lower yourself, keeping your legs bent so you don't touch the floor. From the starting position pull your body up and touch the back of your neck to the bar. Repeat this alternate chinning routine at least three times.

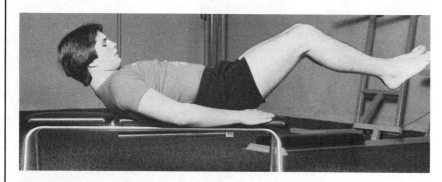

The Bench Press

Begin with one of the classic weight-training exercises, the Bench Press. This exercise works the pectorals, which are the muscles in the chest, and is terrific for warming up the entire upper torso in preparation for arm and shoulder exercises.

Lie on the exercise bench as shown in the first photograph. When you move to the more advanced series I will suggest that you position your legs differently, but in the beginning you need the stability of having your legs spread over the bench and your feet planted firmly on the floor. Grip the bar a few inches wider than your shoulders and hold it above your chest. Slowly lower the bar until it barely touches your chest between your nipples and your neck and then press it slowly back to the top. Let me remind you to use a weight you can handle easily. If you have to struggle and your movements become jerky you have already defeated much of the purpose of the Bench Press.

Inhale as you lower the bar, exhale as you push it back to the top.

Build to 1 set of 10 to 12 reps in the first two weeks, then increase to 2 sets of 10 to 12 reps by eight weeks. After eight weeks maintain the same number of sets and reps and increase the weight on the bar by 2 pounds each week. Suggested starting weight: 30 to 50 pounds.

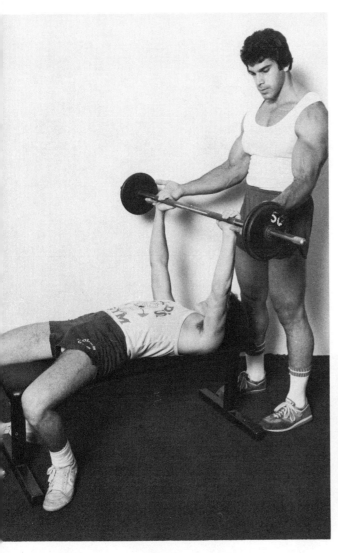

The Dumbbell Curl

Because I do Dumbbell Curls with a slight twist I believe they have a certain advantage for biceps work over curls with a bar.

Stand with your feet spread approximately 16 inches apart and hold the dumbbells against your thighs, palms facing inward. Keeping your upper arms held tightly against your sides, begin lifting the dumbbells and turning them slowly until your palms are facing upward and then curl the dumbbells until they are as close to your chest as possible. Hold this extreme position briefly, concentrating on feeling a full flex in each biceps, and then lower the dumbbells slowly back to the starting position. To isolate your biceps, do not allow your upper arms to move forward or backward. Exhale as you curl the dumbbells, inhale as you lower them back to your thighs.

Build to 1 set of 12 to 15 reps during the first two weeks, increasing to 2 sets of 12 to 15 reps by the end of eight weeks. After eight weeks increase the weight by 2 pounds per week. Suggested starting weight: 10 to 15 pounds each.

The Triceps Extension
with a Dumbbell

Most young bodybuilders concentrate on developing their biceps and neglect their triceps. Remember that great-looking arms and fantastic measurements are achieved by equal development of the total arm, biceps and triceps. The Triceps Extension with a Dumbbell will help bring about that balance.

Hold the dumbbell as shown in the first photograph, keeping your elbows upright and close to your head. Now, without moving your upper arms, lower the dumbbell as far as you can behind your head, allowing for maximum stretch in the triceps. Pause and then lift the dumbbell back to the beginning position. Inhale as you lower the dumbbell, exhale as you lift it.

Begin with 1 set of 12 reps and increase to 2 sets of 15 reps by the end of eight weeks. Add weight gradually and never try to handle too much. Suggested starting weight: 10 to 12 pounds.

The Military Press

The Military Press helps build the broad powerful shoulders that are the identifying mark of a true bodybuilder. This exercise works directly on your deltoids and prepares them for the more specialized movements to come in later programs.

Take a fairly wide grip on the barbell (the photograph will give you the idea), raise it to your chest, pause, then press it above your head. Lower the weight slowly to your chest and press it above your head again. Make sure your movements are slow and smooth, especially as you lower the bar. Do not allow it to come down and bounce off your chest. Exhale as you press, inhale as you lower the weight.

Build to 1 set of 10 reps during the first two weeks, increase to 2 sets of 12 reps by the end of eight weeks. Add 2 pounds weekly — if you can continue to handle it with complete control. Suggested starting weight: 30 to 50 pounds.

Bent-Over Rowing with a Bar

The powerful latissimus dorsi muscles—or lats, as most body-builders call them—give your back that impressive V shape which adds so much to a good physique. One of the most effective exercises for this muscle group is Bent-Over Rowing with a Bar.

Begin with your feet spread approximately 12–16 inches, or shoulder width, apart and your knees slightly bent. Bend at the waist until your back is flat and parallel to the floor and grip the bar a few inches farther apart than your shoulders. Pull the weight to your chest, pause, lower it slowly back to the floor, and repeat. Form is of utmost importance in this exercise. Your back should remain flat; your knees should be bent; only your arms should move.

Build to 1 set of 10 reps during the first two weeks, increase to 2 sets of 12 reps by the end of eight weeks. Add weight slowly—2 to 5 pounds per week—and never sacrifice form for weight. Suggested starting weight: 30 to 50 pounds.

The Squat

I neglected my legs for years and paid heavily for it in my first contests. Since I realized that mistake I have encouraged beginning bodybuilders to work as hard on their legs as they do on their upper bodies. The Squat is a supreme leg exercise, of course, but it is more. It is beneficial to your entire cardiovascular system, helps to expand your rib cage, and also works on the muscles in your buttocks and hip areas.

Stand erect with the bar resting across your shoulders and your heels on a 2 × 4 block. With your eyes straight ahead, your back straight, and your hands balancing the bar, go down until your thighs are parallel to the floor, then rise back to the standing position. Inhale as you go down, exhale as you rise to the standing position. Keep your back straight and do not allow it to swing or wobble during the movements of the exercise. Work slowly and smoothly and do not rush yourself. Add weight only as you can handle it.

Build to 1 set of 10 reps during the first two weeks, increase to 2 sets of 10 to 15 reps by the end of the eighth week. Suggested starting weight: 30 pounds.

The Calf Raise

Although you may not have stopped to think about it, the calf muscles may be the most impressive in the entire body. Look at the treatment given calves by the classical sculptors; they are wide and thick and have a definite heart shape in statues of athletes and gods. In bodybuilding, calves can be the deciding factor in a close competition.

Stand with your feet approximately 12 inches apart, your toes up on a block. To increase the resistance, you may use a barbell, holding it across your shoulders. Stand up on your toes as far as you can go, pause, then slowly lower your heels back to the starting position. Inhale as you go up, exhale as you come down. The greatest benefit comes from a large number of slow, well-stretched reps.

Build to 2 sets of 15 reps in the first two weeks, and increase to 4 sets of 15 reps by the end of eight weeks. Suggested starting weight: 30 to 50 pounds.

The Bent-Knee Sit-up

You should be familiar with this exercise from the earlier section of the book. Turn back and review the movements given on page 145.

By this point you should easily be able to perform 3 or 4 sets of 15 to 30 reps. Build until you are doing a total of 150 to 200 reps.

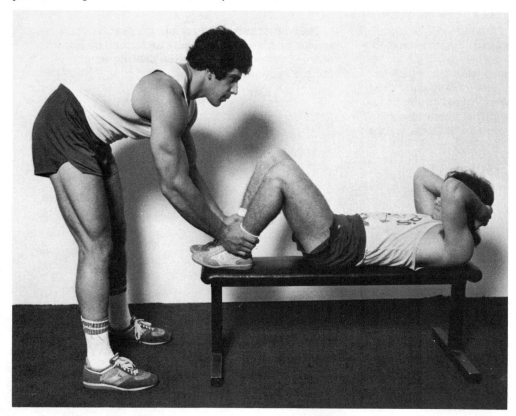

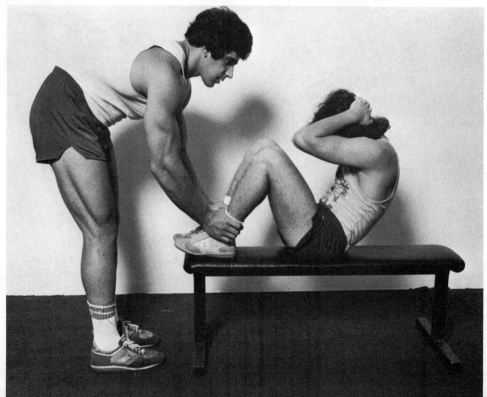

COOLING DOWN

Following my workout I take a few minutes to go through another stretching routine, which I call the cool down. The purpose is to stretch all the muscles I have worked and allow them to relax. No matter how fast or heavy I have trained, I move slowly through the cool-down movements. This allows my heart rate to come down more gradually and lets the flow of blood in my body to normalize itself.

Pulls

I begin with a series of pulls and pushes, which I do by grasping a part of an exercise machine, a door frame, or anything else that is solid enough to allow me to get a good stretch. You should feel this especially through the lats and the muscles in the small of your back. Changing the position of your legs will help get at the leg biceps and calves.

Standing Head to Knees

Holding your legs straight, reach down and take hold of the backs of your ankles and bring your upper body down as far as you can. Ideally, you should be able to touch your head to your legs. However, in the beginning go only as far as you can without straining. Repeat twice more.

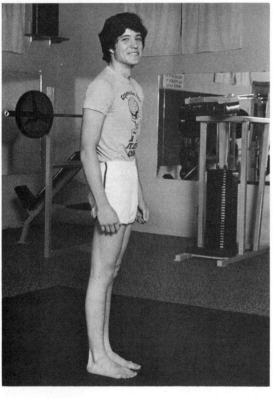

Side Bends

With your hands clasped behind your neck and your feet spread approximately 18 inches apart, bend your upper body as far as you can to the right. Hold the extreme position for a few seconds, then return to the upright position. Do the same thing to the left side. Repeat twice more to each side.

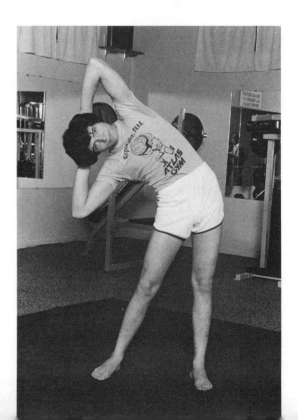

Chest Expansion

A great exercise to free up the chest and most of the upper body is the chest expansion.

Clasp your hands behind your back, then, holding your arms straight, lift as high as you can. Hold to the count of five and lower your hands. Rest a moment, then repeat once.

Seated Head to Knees

Sitting on the floor, your legs extended in front of you, reach out and touch your toes. Hold this for a few seconds, then gradually bring your head as close to your knees as you can. Repeat twice more.

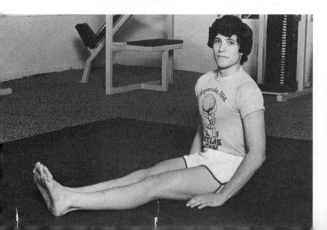

Shoulder Stand

Begin by lying on your back on the floor. Bring your knees up to your chest and roll up onto your shoulders, supporting your back with your hands. Slowly raise your legs until they are extended straight above you. Hold this position as long as you can, breathing normally, or for a total of three minutes.

FROM LOU

The exercises you have just learned are basic, no-nonsense movements that should see you through to the time when your skeletal growth is complete and you can feel secure about going on to more complicated programs and perhaps even to becoming a professional bodybuilder.

Let me remind you again that weight itself is not the name of the game. Be safe. Work with the poundage you can handle easily. If it doesn't seem that you've done enough after 10 or 12 reps, try 15 or 16—that should give you a good burn. Remember that the most effective training is done with slow, smooth, strict movements and that most of the best exercises are simple and direct.

Instead of adding more resistance training exercises to your program I would like to encourage you to combine the exercises I have already given with running, swimming, biking, or any other sport that you particularly enjoy, and in this way keep your weight training fresh, challenging, and special.

6

LOU'S SECRETS FOR COMPETITIVE BODYBUILDING

THE COMPETITIVE BODYBUILDER

Few people in bodybuilding ever have to ask: Should I compete? When you reach that advanced stage you will know it. In fact, if you are as motivated as I was, nothing could prevent you from stepping into the ranks of the professional bodybuilder.

Competitive bodybuilders are the elite in the field and represent a small percentage of the people who engage in weight training for the purpose of health and fitness. They are men and women of special focus and dedication. If you are among them you will already have worked your way through the previous chapters, discovered your strong and weak points, and set up your own unique program of balance and refinement.

At this point in your life, training becomes a personal thing. The small differences in bodies, how they react to food and respond to exercise, are extremely important to any bodybuilder going into competitive training. You must be totally in touch with your body, knowing when to change your diet, knowing if and when you should use such advanced training methods as supersets and giant sets (explained later in this chapter). This knowledge of your body and its idiosyncrasies will make the difference between success and failure when you stand before the judges' table.

TIMING

Your body cannot be pushed to the limit and maintain its peak for a long period of time. For most people the ultimate 100 percent peak of condition is reached after three to five months of intense training and can be held at this level for no more than seven to ten days. Trial and error will tell you how long your body takes, what kind of training programs bring it to the peak in the least amount of time, and how you should maintain it. For these reasons it makes sense to choose no more than two or three contests per year and give them all your energy. Remember that competing is a great experience but winning is what you are after.

Cycles

I have a theory that the best and most effective program for the competitive bodybuilder is to work in carefully calculated cycles. My complete cycle (your own times will be relative to how your body responds) consists of what I call my off-season phase, which is from six weeks to four months, and my precontest phase, which is from four to six weeks. During the off-season phase I hold down the pace, work with fairly heavy weights, and concentrate on doing mostly basic movements. The precontest phase is much faster, with emphasis on definition and muscle hardness through cheating, forced reps, and concentration on negative movements.

YOUR PERSONAL ROUTINE

By this time in your career most of you will have begun to formulate the routine best suited for your own body. Stay in tune with your feelings, but also ask for advice and help from more experienced bodybuilders. Reading books and attending seminars can provide information and ideas that you may never encounter through your efforts in the gym. I should like to suggest a few rules for making the most progress in the least amount of time.

1. Never train more than two to two and a half hours each day.
2. Never do more than 16 sets per muscle group in an off-season training day and never more than 20 sets in a precontest training day.
3. Always include at least one basic exercise per body part along with the shaping and defining movements you do during your precontest training sessions.
4. Do abdominals and calves first in your precontest routine as a warm-up.
5. Do arms *after* your torso or on a separate day.
6. Save forearm training until the last period of each day, because after a hard forearm workout you will have difficulty grasping the bar.
7. Priority training—to blast those lagging muscles—should be done early in the workout or on a different day.

TRAINING TIPS

FORCED REPS

My favorite technique for pushing a muscle to its ultimate, once it has reached the point of failure, is forced reps. During off-season training I use them only in the final set for each muscle group, but in precontest work I employ the technique in every set except my warm-up set. The easiest example to give is the Bench

Press. I like to work with over 400 pounds for 5 full reps and then have my training partner step in to assist me by lifting the equivalent of perhaps 20 pounds, allowing me to force out another 2 or 3 reps.

USING NEGATIVES

We have known for years that making use of negative resistance in a weight-training exercise can be as effective as making use of positive resistance and that the negatives often develop parts of a muscle that are left untouched by just concentrating on the more conventional positive movements.

Really effective negative sets take special work—on your part and on the part of two partners. Once you are warmed up with one or two sets of conventional movements in which you have concentrated on taking advantage of the negative phase of the exercise, load your bar or machine with 50 percent more weight than you were just using in the positive/negative sets. Have your partners help you through the positive phase and then allow you to resist the downward movement of the bar or machine for from 5 to 8 reps. Stop the set when you can no longer control the downward force of the weight.

Using the pure negative technique given above, perform no more than one workout per week for each body part.

SPLIT ROUTINES

During the precontest phase of my training I train each major body part three times a week on a six-day split routine. I recommend that calves be trained every day and forearms at least five times a week. There are a number of ways to split your body parts for training. The following are two split routines that have worked for me:

1. MONDAY, WEDNESDAY, FRIDAY: chest, back, shoulders, calves, abs, forearms.
   TUESDAY, THURSDAY, SATURDAY: thighs, biceps, triceps, calves, abs, forearms.
2. MONDAY, WEDNESDAY, FRIDAY: chest, shoulders, triceps, lower back, calves, abs, forearms.
   TUESDAY, THURSDAY, SATURDAY: thighs, upper back, biceps, forearms, calves, abs.

Your own split routine will depend on a number of variables, including priority training and how your body responds best to a particular split. Remember that what works for me won't necessarily work for you.

SUPERSETS

Many bodybuilders use the superset technique as a part of regular advanced programs. For me, however, supersets were only really effective during the final two or three weeks before a contest. They helped me harden up, but if I used them over a longer period of time I began to lose size.

A superset consists of two exercises done consecutively with only five to ten seconds rest between them and a rest of forty-five seconds to a minute before the next superset. Supersets can be done for opposing muscle groups (probably the most effective) or for the same muscle group.

Examples of opposing-group supersets:

BICEPS/TRICEPS: Barbell Curl, Triceps Press-down
CHEST/BACK: Bench Press, Chins
QUADS/HAMSTRINGS: Leg Extension, Leg Curl

Examples of same-group supersets:

BICEPS/BICEPS: Preacher Curl, Barbell Curl
CHEST/CHEST: Bench Press, Flyes
CALVES/CALVES: Seated Calf Raise, Donkey Calf Raise

TRISETS AND GIANT SETS

These are extensions of the superset principle. Trisets consist of three exercises done consecutively with no rest between them; they can be done for three body parts or for different areas of the muscles in a single body part. Giant sets are the ultimate extension of supersetting, consisting of four or five exercises with minimal rest between them. These techniques are strictly for final hardening up and should be used for only two or three weeks prior to competition.

POSING

Posing is both an art and a science, involving almost as much mathematics as pure feeling. You become a dancer, an actor, a salesman. Again, the key is knowing your body and how best to present it—first to maximize your strong points and second to minimize your weak points.

Learning to pose and present your body in the best possible manner is one of the most important parts of successful professional bodybuilding. Long before you plan to enter your first competition you should be formulating your posing routine and practicing it every day. Poses should be chosen depending on how they feel to you, how they look to you (always pose before a mirror), and how they look to other, more experienced professional

Winning the Mr. Universe title for the second time, Verona, Italy, 1974

bodybuilders. Remember this: Posing should not be static. Each pose should flow gracefully into the next so that your routine becomes a kind of performance. There are a number of sources for poses—magazines, books, films, and actual contests. I suggest that you always remain open to new poses that will enhance your routine and that you can put in the place of less effective poses.

During the final four to six weeks before a contest I work on my posing for an hour or two each day. I use this time not only to improve my routine but to help me achieve my contest finish. This period of flexing, which is based on what I call the iso-tension principle, actually makes my muscles harder and gives them more definition.

Music was difficult for me in the first few contests because I could not hear it that well. However, since I have been wearing improved hearing aids I realize how much music adds to the overall character of a strong routine. You should choose your music with a number of things in mind—the way it fits your overall appearance (are you rugged or more refined?), how familiar it is to the audience, and how it works with the rhythm and movement of your own posing routine. My personal feeling is that music for posing should be both lyrical and powerful, that it should be full of rich highs and lows, and that it should give your routine a professional, tailored look.

PRECONTEST GROOMING

A few weeks before a contest you should start the cosmetic treatments that will prepare you for competing. Five or six weeks prior to a contest I shave all my body hair and then keep it trimmed close with an electric shaver. A week before the contest I get my hair cut and shaped. A big, bushy head of hair can take away from the size of your shoulders, arms, and chest. Unless you have maintained your tan over a long period of time you should give yourself at least six weeks to build up good color. A short period every day is much better than risking a bad sunburn by being out too long.

IT'S YOUR SHOW

What I have said in these pages about competitive bodybuilding is only as good as the use you make of it. From this point on it is up to you. Your confidence, diligence, talent, drive, desire, and vision will determine what kind of life you will have in this sport. I can only wish you the best and encourage you to accept every challenge and go into each competition with the true feeling of sportsmanship.

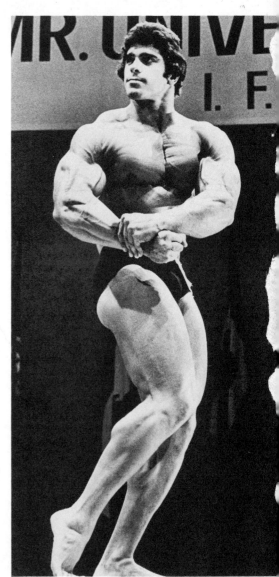

Mr. Universe Contest, 1974

208